"In *Grasping for the American Dream*, Taplin-Kaguru describes the African Americans she interviewed as being on a treadmill. Running, exhausted, sometimes for years, trying to grasp the just-out-of-reach American Dream promised by homeownership. Census data and other quantitative studies have shown the countless ways in which homeownership simply looks different for African Americans due to racist policies and practices that created decades of segregation, disinvestment, and exploitation. But Taplin-Kaguru's qualitative study brings those numbers to life and shows the human impact of creating an American Dream tied to homeownership, and then systematically denying that Dream—or putting it just out of reach—to generations of African Americans. The stories of the people she interviewed revealed an often deep commitment to homeownership as a signal of adult accomplishment and a source of freedom, even as structural barriers associated with such things as credit scores and student loans made the Dream elusive and delayed at best. Taplin-Kaguru deftly weaves this narrative together, drawing on sociological expertise and the voices of her subjects, to create an important contribution in the new line of research focused on understanding the lived experiences of individuals as they seek housing. Taplin-Kaguru interviewed people over several years and focused on an often-overlooked group—the black working class. The result is a rich and nuanced understanding of both the desire to achieve the Dream and the structural barriers to realizing it. Barriers that leave these home seekers stuck on the treadmill."

Maria Krysan, Professor of Sociology, University of Illinois at Chicago, and co-author of *Cycle of Segregation: Social Processes and Residential Stratification*

"This masterful work of scholarship, written in a graceful and inviting style, builds on exemplary urban studies, such as those by Herb Gans, Karyn Lacy, and Mary Pattillo. It uniquely follows sixty-eight working-class and lower-middle-class African Americans in the Chicago metropolitan area through the process of buying a home, some of whom were not successful. The fine-grained results are enriched by a follow-up survey with thirty-eight of those who made a purchase, and by interviews with several of the former neighbors of the new homeowners. The result is impressive evidence for the endurance of the African American Dream of freedom, equality, and integration against all odds, a dream that ironically makes potential homebuyers 'more vulnerable to exploitation in a structurally racist housing market.' This book, including poignant accounts of how the disappointments in the face of ongoing racial discrimination are dealt with by a determined and resilient group of people, is destined to take its place on the shelf of classic urban studies."

G. William Domhoff, Distinguished Professor Emeritus and Research Professor in Sociology, University of California, Santa Cruz, author of *Who Rules America?*

"Despite being exploited and abused by the economics and policies of homeownership time and time again, Black Americans continue to uphold homebuying as a core component of their respectability, citizenship, and defiance of racism's setbacks. Nora Taplin-Kaguru fills in so many of the missing pieces of how and why Black homebuyers face these purchasing obstacles and ultimately gives voice to their reasons, their considerations, and how they make sense of a process that has historically marginalized Black communities."

Saida Grundy, Assistant Professor of Sociology and African American studies at Boston University, and the author of the forthcoming *Manhood within the Margins: Promise, Peril and Paradox at the Historically Black College for Men*

GRASPING FOR THE AMERICAN DREAM

African American homebuyers continue to pay more for and get less from homeownership. This book explains the motivations for pursuing homeownership among working-class African Americans despite the structural conditions that make it less economically and socially rewarding for this group. Fervent adherence to the American Dream ideology among working-class African Americans makes them more vulnerable to exploitation in a structurally racist housing market. The book draws on qualitative interviews with sixty-eight African American aspiring homebuyers looking to buy a home in the Chicago metropolitan area to investigate the housing-search process and residential relocation decisions in the context of a racially segregated metropolitan region.

Working-class African Americans remained committed to homeownership, in part because of the moral status attached to achieving this goal. For African American homebuyers, success at the American Dream of homeownership is directly related to the long-standing dream of equality. For the aspiring homebuyers in this study, delayed homeownership was a practical problem for the same reasons, but they also experienced this as a personal failing, due to the strong cultural expectation in the United States that homeownership is a milestone that middle-class adults must achieve. Furthermore, despite using perfectly reasonable housing search strategies to locate homes in stable or improving racially integrated neighborhoods, the structure of racial segregation limits their agency in housing choices. Ultimately, policy solutions will need to address structural racism broadly and be attuned to the needs of both homeowners and renters.

Nora E. Taplin-Kaguru is Assistant Professor of Sociology at Earlham College. She is an urban sociologist, studying racism, housing, the built environment and social media. She has also been published in *City & Community*.

NEW CRITICAL VIEWPOINTS ON SOCIETY SERIES

Edited by Joe R. Feagin

Got Solidarity?
Challenging Straight White College Men to Advocate for Social Justice
Jörg Vianden

Love Under the Skin
Interracial Marriages in the American South and France
Cécile Coquet-Mokoko

Through an Artist's Eyes
The Dehumanization and Racialization of Jews and Political Dissidents during the Third Reich
Willa M. Johnson

Leveraging Multigenerational Workforce Strategies in Higher Education
Edna Chun and Alvin Evans

Grasping for the American Dream
Racial Segregation, Social Mobility, and Homeownership
Nora E. Taplin-Kaguru

Who Killed Higher Education?
Maintaining White Dominance in a Desegregation Era
Edna B. Chun and Joe R. Feagin

For more information about this series, please visit www.routledge.com/New-Critical-Viewpoints-on-Society/book-series/NCVS

GRASPING FOR THE AMERICAN DREAM

Racial Segregation, Social Mobility, and Homeownership

Nora E. Taplin-Kaguru

Routledge
Taylor & Francis Group
NEW YORK AND LONDON

First published 2022
by Routledge
605 Third Avenue, New York, NY 10158

and by Routledge
2 Park Square, Milton Park, Abingdon, Oxon OX14 4RN

Routledge is an imprint of the Taylor & Francis Group, an informa business

Library of Congress Cataloging-in-Publication Data
Names: Taplin-Kaguru, Nora E., author.
Title: Grasping for the American dream : racial segregation, social
mobility, and homeownership / Nora E. Taplin-Kaguru.
Description: New York, NY: Routledge, 2021. |
Includes bibliographical references.
Identifiers: LCCN 2020053751 | ISBN 9780367075927 (hardback) |
ISBN 9780367075941 (paperback) | ISBN 9780429021466 (ebook)
Subjects: LCSH: Discrimination in housing–United States. | African Americans–Housing. |
Home ownership–United States. | Housing–United States–Finance. |
African Americans–Segregation–United States. | African Americans–Social conditions.
Classification: LCC HD7288.76.U5 T36 2021 | DDC 333.33/808996073–dc23
LC record available at https://lccn.loc.gov/2020053751

ISBN: 978-0-367-07592-7 (hbk)
ISBN: 978-0-367-07594-1 (pbk)
ISBN: 978-0-429-02146-6 (ebk)

Typeset in Bembo
by Newgen Publishing UK

To the memory of my grandmother Lois Gougis Taplin Bronz
and for my daughter Wangui Irene Kaguru

CONTENTS

FIGURES

TABLES

ACKNOWLEDGMENTS

This book would not have been possible without the aspiring homeowners who gave their time, and welcomed me into their homes and their lives. I cannot thank the homebuyers in this study enough for selflessly sharing their dreams with me and allowing me to write about their stories. It was a joy to get to know these homebuyers and their families. Their determination is inspiring and continues to bring me hope.

I am also deeply indebted to the housing counselors at Neighborhood Housing Services and the West Cook Homeownership Center who helped me recruit the homebuyers. The housing counselors at these organizations work tirelessly to help families avoid terrible pitfalls that have led many aspiring homebuyers to financial ruin. Through patient and time-consuming work, they help many individuals achieve their American Dream. These housing counselors are stretched far too thin with the demand for services from both aspiring homebuyers and distressed homeowners trying to stay in their homes. Despite their busy schedules filled with this pressing work, Flo Bernard, Sandra Wells, and Sherry Smith of NHS, and Mirna Rodriguez of WCHC made time for me to recruit at their classes.

This book began as my dissertation, under the guidance of my generous advisor John Levi Martin. He was my main source of support since this project was a couple of paragraphs I wrote about the weirdness of Chicago's Black population loss in the 2010 census. He encouraged me to pursue a rigorous research design and to see it through at times when it seemed impossible. He has patiently read countless drafts as this project developed into a dissertation, and then from a dissertation into a book. I am so lucky to have such an excellent sociologist and writer as a mentor, who impressed on me the importance of thinking deeply about the ethics of my project, the validity of my data, the logic of my analysis, and the clarity of my prose. At the University of Chicago, the other members of my committee—Kathleen Cagney, Forrest Stuart, and Scott Allard—also provided invaluable support throughout the development of this project. So many other faculty there helped to shape me as a scholar, including Kimberly Hoang, Mario Small, Omar McRoberts, Terry N. Clark, and the late Richard Taub. The Division of Social Sciences and the Office of Multicultural Student Affairs provided financial support for this research. And many of my fellow graduate students helped me to hone my ideas for this project and to develop strategies for research, including Kathryn Hendricks, Maude Pugliese, Eva Swyngedouw, Thomas Swerts, Maria Akchurin, Nidia Bañuelos, Elizabeth K. Gray, Alicia Riley, Alexandra Brewer, Anjanette M. Chan Tack, Monica Lee, Cayce C. Hughes, Jessica Zulema Borja, Theresa Anasti, and Marcelle M. Medford.

During the two years following my PhD that I spent as a Teaching Post-Doctoral Fellow in the Social Sciences at the University of Chicago, I enjoyed the camaraderie of fellow post-docs as I worked on developing this project further, including Basil Salem, Daniel Nichanian, and Tania M. Jenkins.

This work also benefited greatly from many discussions over the last few years with the University of Illinois Sociology Department Neighborhoods, Housing and Urban Sociology Reading Group. I am grateful to Maria Krysan for taking me under her wing when I was in the early stages of this project and inviting me into this fun and stimulating group. Her encouragement and the advice from her and other NHUS members, including Deanna Christianson, Allison Suppan Helmuth, Maximilian Cuddy, and Eike Marten, have greatly strengthened this work.

Additionally, Marisa Novara and Breann Gala and others at the Metropolitan Planning Council were very helpful as I developed the research design for this project. Working at MPC gave me insight into how professionals in the field look at these housing issues. Through MPC, I met Becca Goldstein at Neighborhood Housing Services of Chicago, who granted me access to the homebuyer education classes without which this research would not have been possible. I am also very grateful to Rob Breymaier and Marz Timms, who granted me access to similar classes at the West Cook Homeownership Center. By attending these classes, I was able to gain access to homebuyers during their decision-making process, which was key to the success of this project. Furthermore, I gained important background information about the homebuying process from my time at these courses.

I could not have found a more supportive and nurturing environment to complete this project than the community of scholar-teachers I found at Earlham College. My colleagues there provided everything from advice on how to manage teaching and research as an assistant professor, to detailed feedback on drafts, and a sounding board for ideas. I am particularly grateful for the support I received from colleagues in Sociology and Anthropology—JoAnn Martin, Victor Kumar, Daniel Rosenberg, Callie Maidhof, Jennifer Cardinal, Vaibhav Saria, and Peter Carlo Becerra —and from others across the college, including Amanda Gray, Elizabeth Schroeder Schlabach, Ryan Patrick Murphy, Michelle Tong, Womai I. Song, Elizabeth Angowski, Eric J. Cunningham, Tiffany Hong, Belén Villarreal,

James Logan, Robert Couch, Karla Fribley, and Jose-Ignacio Pareja. I am also grateful to the college for extensive material support for completing the project. Furthermore, nothing speaks more profoundly to opportunity to conduct high-level research at small liberal arts colleges than the generative relationships I have had with our highly engaged undergraduate students during my time at Earlham. I am especially grateful for my two brilliant undergraduate research assistants, Daniel Oluwasetemi Oni and Della Walters, who helped to bring this project to fruition in so many ways, including helpful comments on making the prose more accessible and creating some beautiful maps.

I thank the anonymous reviewers of this manuscript for their detailed and constructive comments, as well as Dean Birkenkamp and everyone at Routledge who helped to bring this book together. I would also like to express my gratitude for the anonymous reviewers of my *City & Community* article based on this study, whose feedback helped me to clarify the overall project. Also, thank you to *City & Community* for kindly granting permission to reprint portions of "Mobile but Stuck: Multigenerational Neighborhood Decline and Housing Search Strategies for African Americans".

As the daughter of an Irish American who grew up in the leafy Chicago suburb of Lake Forest and an African American of the civil rights generation who left New Orleans to seek opportunities in the North, my quirky multicultural family gave me the perspective that shaped this book and my sociological work generally. My Catholic, Jewish, Irish American, Black, and Creole family members made me who I am and also provided the web of love and support that has made all of my work possible.

My mother always said I was lucky to have a family that appreciated that I am book smart and it's true. I am eternally grateful for the hard work, encouragement, assistance, and guidance of my parents, Edgar Louis Taplin, Jr. and Mary Irene McMahon Taplin. My sweet younger brother Edgar Louis "Buck" Taplin, III, my oldest friend, has provided emotional support and a healthy mix of teasing and acceptance for his nerdy older sister. My aunts, uncles, and cousins, by blood and marriage, real and fictive, the McMahons, Leahys, Shortses, Heberts, Kubotas, Burkes, Becks, Marinos, Bronzes, Beshores, Wanjohis, Mainas and Waciumas have been there for me all along the way as well. In particular, my uncle Dan Burke provided valuable introductions to organizations that were helpful in developing this project. And this project would have been very difficult without some essential help from my cousin Drew McMahon in teaching me how to drive just in time for me to start conducting interviews all over the metropolitan area. It turns out that sometimes the book-smart must learn practical skills in order to write a book!

There are no words for how much this work—and all that I do—has benefited from my marriage to William Kaguru Wanjohi. Bill has been with me since the very beginning of my sociological career, mulling over all my thoughts about interviews and sources as they come up, and discussing every idea that I have had. I do not know what this process would have been like without him providing encouragement when the work seemed overwhelming, being there to celebrate every step closer to making this book a reality and being an incredible partner in parenting our daughter Wangui Irene Kaguru.

I was pregnant with Wangui Irene as I wrote the first full draft of the book, finishing it when she was just a few months old, sometimes writing with her asleep in my lap. I completed the final drafts of this book while our nanny Montana Bennington and my mother kept Wangui Irene happy, healthy, and entertained.

Finally, this book is dedicated to the memory of my grandmother Lois Gougis Taplin Bronz, and to my daughter's future. My grandmother, an African American woman from New Orleans, was once a young widow with three children in the Jim Crow South. She struggled against the odds to make the American Dream possible for our family, for my father who worked to hold onto it for me, but she did not stop there. She dedicated herself to the fight for civil rights, for fair and affordable housing, and for a more accessible dream for all. It is my deepest wish that this book contributes in some tiny way to her legacy and to my daughter living in a better, more just world.

1

TIFFANY'S STORY

> Bronzeville—that part of Chicago's South Side where 300,000 Negroes live—is something that should not exist—an area set aside for the halting use of a single race. ("Here thou, and thou alone shalt stay: and no place other.") However, since a Bronzeville does exist, it is satisfying to demonstrate that here resides essentially only what is ordinary: human struggle, human whimsicality, and human reach toward soul-settlement, toward peace if not happiness, sufficiency if not fortune.
>
> *(Gwendolyn Brooks, "They Call it Bronzeville," 1951)*

Bronzeville was a destination neighborhood for African Americans during the Great Migration (1910–1970). In the early 20th century, it was the center of Black political and economic life as well as arts and culture in Chicago. Bronzeville is also geographically central to Black life in Chicago, sitting at the core of Chicago's historic Black Belt. It is an unofficial neighborhood name that crosses two official Chicago community areas: Grand Boulevard and Douglas. Along with New York's Harlem, this was an important site for the early development of Black mass cultural industries including music, film, and beauty, and was uniquely situated at the core of the "Black metropolis," as studied by sociologists St. Clair Drake and Horace R. Cayton, and recognized by historians as central to the national development of Black economic, cultural, and social life (Baldwin 2007, Schlabach 2012). The neighborhood had a complicated recent history, though. During the latter half of the 20th century, deindustrialization, the construction of public housing towers, and middle-class Black flight turned Bronzeville into an area of concentrated poverty. But in the 2000s, Bronzeville experienced a resurgence of development. Housing prices soared in the neighborhood during these boom years. Most newcomers to the neighborhood during this time were Black and middle-class. Many of them bought homes with subprime loans. Subsequently, the neighborhood was one of the hardest hit by the housing bust in 2008 and foreclosure crisis of the Great Recession (2007–2009).

In the summer of 2015, I interviewed Tiffany, a nail technician in her late thirties. She was renting a beautiful apartment in a Bronzeville condo building where she lived with her one son. The renovated apartment had fashionable

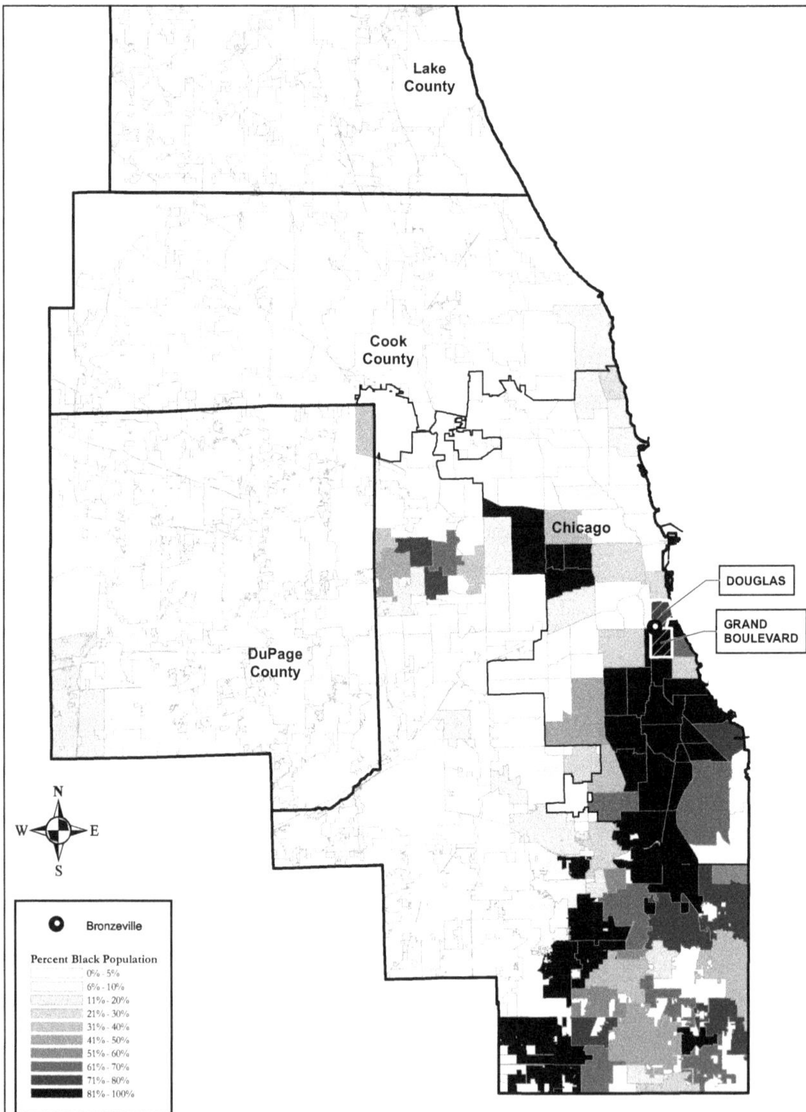

FIGURE 1.1 Map of Douglas and Grand Boulevard

features: exposed brick walls, hardwood floors, and an open kitchen with new stainless-steel appliances. The renovated kitchen and other recent updates to the space were clearly vestiges of the 2000s housing boom. Tiffany liked the area for its "historic qualities" and for the fact that it is "still developing." Tiffany explained that the owner of the unit she dwelled in "purchased on the higher end of the market" and "needs to sell it." Tiffany was renting the apartment from the condo owner with the aid of a housing choice voucher (HCV), a federally funded housing rental subsidy. One of her reasons for considering buying a home was that her income was increasing, and she was on the cusp of ineligibility for the HCV. At the time of our interview, Tiffany was considering buying the unit via the Chicago Housing Authority (CHA) Choose to Own program, which provides assistance for HCV recipients to move out of the program and into homeownership. Moreover, for a brief time after Tiffany was born (more than three decades ago), her family had lived in the city and attended a church near her current apartment in Bronzeville. When Tiffany was two years old, her parents bought a house in the suburb of Riverdale, Illinois, just south of Chicago.

This book is about African American aspiring homebuyers like Tiffany, whose family histories and personal experiences traverse geographic and political boundaries between cities and suburbs. Metropolitan areas better represent the regions in which people live and search for housing than do particular municipalities. For that reason, I followed the stories of homebuyers across the metropolitan area (and even included a few who left for other parts of the country).

When Tiffany's family moved to Riverdale, it was a working-class, racially integrated suburb. Tiffany painted a picture of a bucolic childhood in Riverdale:

> Manicured lawns, everybody was friendly. I remember being free to walk in the neighborhood and go to the store at probably seven, eight years old. It was very safe. My mother and father, they put us in the public school, which was on the next block, and we could walk there, and there were no issues, and it was a very good school.

Tiffany began to notice changes around the time that she graduated from high school in 1999—the lawns had deteriorated, there were more abandoned buildings, and the grocery store closed. She heard about the increasing frequency of break-ins in the neighborhood and even occasional shootings. She was concerned for her mother, who was still living there in the house where she grew up:

> She was a pioneer and she's like, "I'm going to be the last one standing." I hate that that's the case because now she really couldn't get much for her place if she wanted to.

Tiffany's mother was a racial "pioneer," one of the first African Americans to move into a White neighborhood. At the time, it appeared that she had achieved the quintessential American Dream of suburban homeownership, but neighborhood decline has diminished her achievement.

Riverdale has experienced population loss, and the ensuing property tax burden has increased on the remaining homeowners, while housing values have declined (the median house sales price declined 76% from 2006 to 2016). It has also experienced severe White flight. Riverdale went from 40% Black in 1990 to 93% Black in 2010 (US Census Bureau 1990, 2000, 2010). Between Tiffany's childhood home of Riverdale and her condo in Bronzeville, she has been followed by problems of neighborhood decline, racial segregation, and resegregation. Ultimately, persistent racial segregation has followed her from the city to the suburbs, and back to the city again. Although the effects of racial segregation have made homeownership a particularly risky proposition for Tiffany, it is still a goal that Tiffany and many other African Americans are interested in pursuing.

When I last interviewed Tiffany three years later in 2018, she still had not purchased a home. During that time, she vacillated between thinking she should continue renting, move out of state, or buy her condo in Bronzeville. During that last interview, she was feeling good about the prospect of buying a home in Bronzeville again, despite both the challenges she knew Bronzeville had faced in recent years and her parents' experience of neighborhood decline due to White flight in the suburb where they had bought her childhood home. She said of Bronzeville: "I see a lot of beautiful homes being built, condos in my area, and I see a lot of diversity as well. I really like that. So, I'm excited for the community." Tiffany retained hope that Bronzeville could have another rebirth—one characterized by increased racial integration—and that she could successfully attain homeownership in a way that would bolster her middle-class status.

To understand why African Americans with stories like Tiffany's would still be interested in purchasing a home, we have to consider the meaning of owning your own home in America, particularly for African Americans. This meaning transcends economic value alone. Without a doubt, housing provides many things of value, including shelter, a basic and indispensable human need. The location of one's housing also determines access to community and various location-based resources. In the United States, housing also has been a means to build wealth and has represented the basis for the American middle class. To this end, mass homeownership has been supported through a variety of government benefits. One of the largest of these is the federal mortgage interest deduction, which is estimated to cost about $70 billion per year (Turner et al. 2013). Government support encourages Americans to use homeownership as a vehicle for saving money. Housing equity makes up a large share of household net worth for all racial groups in the United States—and an even greater share of assets for Black families compared to White families—despite the fact that Black households have lower levels of housing equity in absolute terms (Sullivan et al. 2015).

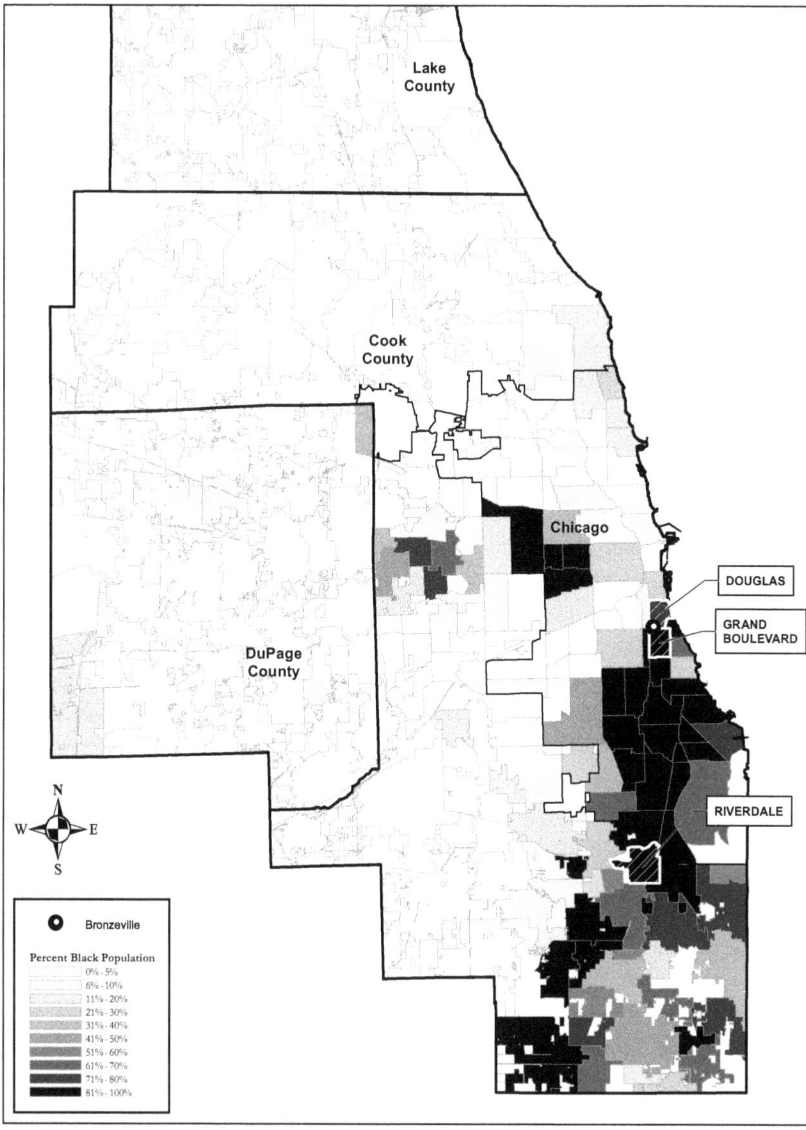

FIGURE 1.2 Map of Grand Boulevard, Douglas, and Riverdale

Overall, African Americans get less economic value out of homeownership than other groups in the United States. The exclusion of African Americans from this core part of American middle-class life has been an essential part of the system of racial inequality in this country. Furthermore, this exclusion has implications, not just for the financial resources available to Black communities, but also for separation from mainstream American life and a denial of full inclusion in citizenship. This long-standing and persistent marginalization in the area of homeownership contributes to a variety of other racial disparities, including those in education and health, as well as employment and the criminal justice system. African Americans simultaneously pay more for a home compared to Whites, and get less in return. For example, African Americans on average pay one-third of a percentage point more on mortgage interest rates than Whites. In practice, this means that an African American homebuyer purchasing a median-priced home in 1999 would typically pay over $11,000 more in interest over the course of a 30-year loan. Additionally, due to racial bias in housing markets, African Americans earn less equity in their homes. The median wealth return to homeownership for Black families is about 25% lower than the median wealth return to White families from homeownership (Shapiro 2004). Despite paying more and getting less, many African Americans want to buy homes. Camille Zubrinsky Charles (2006) found that in the Los Angeles area 64% of non-owning Blacks aspired to buy a home compared with about half of non-owning Whites.

Given this situation, why does homeownership continue to be an ideal for African Americans? How do African Americans approach the home-buying process in this context of disadvantage? African Americans pursue homeownership despite these challenges, because it represents the African American Dream of freedom and equality. While African Americans are often accused of having an alternative ideology, I argue that the fervent adherence of working-class African Americans to the American Dream ideology actually makes them more vulnerable to exploitation in a structurally racist housing market. My findings among homebuyers are similar to what Michaela Soyer (2016) found among juvenile defendants—that their deep belief in the American Dream actually makes it more difficult to navigate situations in which they are at a tremendous structural disadvantage.

While the meaning of homeownership is thoroughly intertwined with a more general idea of the American Dream, for African Americans homeownership represents a particular version of this dream and carries extra weight. The achievement of homeownership symbolizes full citizenship and inclusion in mainstream American life for African Americans who have been historically excluded from full citizenship. Many African Americans also see neighborhood racial integration as an important aspect of this dream and the ability to buy into a racially integrated neighborhood marks achievement under the terms of this dream. Finally, homeowner status is also a moral status imbued with a sense of respectability and middle-class success. Achieving this status is seen as one way to undermine negative stereotypes applied to Black people. The moral importance of homeownership makes it all the more painful that working-class African Americans who are actively pursuing homeownership through reasonable strategies continually find their goals thwarted by structural constraints.

In this book, I examine how working-class African American homebuyers understand their own roles in navigating the homebuying process in a racially segregated metropolitan region. Since America's most hypersegregated areas are large metropolitan areas in the Midwest, I used the Chicago metropolitan area as my site for studying this phenomenon. To be sure, though, these cases point to much larger phenomena that Black homebuyers and those aspiring to homeownership are experiencing across the nation. While this study began in 2014, the context of the Trump presidency and the multifaceted economic struggles occurring during the COVID-19 pandemic have further highlighted these issues. I have grounded this book in in-depth interviews with sixty-eight African American aspiring homebuyers (from sixty-five separate households) and follow-up data from thirty-eight of the homebuyers collected over the course of four years. These aspiring homebuyers were mostly working-class to lower-middle-class. The follow-up data includes in-person interviews, ethnographic observation of home viewings, and brief phone interviews. By following homebuyers over time, I was able to capture what led them to pursue homeownership, their decision-making process, and how they understood the outcomes of their search.

Housing matters because it is a key resource that mediates household access to other goods. Research on place-based inequality has uncovered the ways that racial residential segregation creates entrenched, systemic conditions that further racial inequality (Sharkey 2013). Residential segregation increases economic, educational, and environmental inequality (Massey and Denton 1993; Shapiro 2004). Why talk about racial segregation or its opposite, racial integration? Does positing racial integration as a necessary good suggest that Black spaces or Black people are somehow "naturally" deficient (Pattillo 2019)? While some arguments for integration fall into this trap of stigmatizing Black spaces and by extension Black people, there are other reasons to defend integration as a goal. For instance, Sherrilyn Ifill (2019) argues that we should acknowledge "the pragmatic reality that housing integration may be the most foolproof way to ensure the equitable allocation of public services and development dollars for black children and families" (35). Racial segregation must be dismantled because this structure enables the unequal distribution of resources along racial lines. It is a foundation for a system of racial oppression. Black neighborhoods and neighborhoods experiencing White flight do not suffer because Black people do not bring resources to their neighborhoods, but because a racially biased housing system creates the conditions for wealth extraction from Black families, for exploitation that steals wealth from Black communities, especially across generations (Satter 2009). One important consequence of racial housing inequality is the racial wealth gap. While the income gap between Blacks and Whites is shrinking, the wealth gap is actually continuing to grow. The median household net worth of White households is thirteen times greater than that of Black households and much of this is attributable to differences in housing equity (Shapiro 2004).

Furthermore, the housing crisis brought to the forefront the fact that African Americans who historically had more limited access to home loans were now facing a new type of discrimination. The foreclosure crisis disproportionately affected African American households, and this process led to a hardening of racial segregation (Hall, Crowder, and Spring 2015). Partly because of this crisis, from 1990 to 2015 homeownership rates fell for White, Black, and Hispanic people aged 35 to 44 years old. But the homeownership rate for Blacks in this age group dropped to half the level of homeownership for Whites of the same age and to a lower rate than Black homeownership in 1960 (Goodman, Zhu, and Pendall 2017). Rather than denying access to credit, banks were disproportionately selling to African Americans loans with terrible terms. These predatory lending practices caused lasting harm to African American families and wreaked havoc on Black neighborhoods.

This study shows how working-class African American aspiring homeowners have responded to the housing crisis and ongoing demographic shifts in their search for new homes. The housing crisis had a broader effect beyond the devastating financial cost to those who were directly harmed. The crisis disproportionately affected predominately Black communities, bringing with it all the problems associated with mass foreclosures. Furthermore, I found that homeownership carries moral and social importance that transcends financial benefits. In short, those who lost their homeowner status also lost the social standing that goes with it. Communities that lost their homeowners were torn apart by this crisis in a variety of ways. For African Americans, the housing crisis was interpreted as a moral crisis and a major setback for progress towards equal standing as American citizens.

This book focuses on the experience of housing disadvantage for African American homebuyers. While other groups experience disadvantage in this context, Black peoples' experiences of housing injustice in the United States are unique in many ways and warrant their own discussion. It should also be noted that Black people are not a monolithic group in American cities or suburbs. For instance, Orly Clergé (2019) explains how Black immigrants from Africa and the Caribbean often share suburban communities with descendants of enslaved Black people in the United States, forging complex relationships across these diasporic identities. While the homebuyers in this study were mostly African Americans with long histories in the United States, originating in the experience of racial slavery, a few were more recent immigrants from the Caribbean.

While other non-White racial groups are also residentially segregated to some degree, White–Black segregation is more extreme than levels of segregation experienced by any other groups. Charles (2006) found that a racial hierarchy of preference for neighbors exists among non-Hispanic Blacks, Whites, and Asians, as well as Latinos, with Blacks starkly at the bottom of the hierarchy and Whites at the top. As part of the immigration adaption process, Latinos and Asians typically assimilate and perpetuate the racial negative stereotypes about Blacks common in the United States—and this informs neighborhood preferences. Phenotypically

Black Hispanics also experience high levels of segregation, more similar to that experienced by non-Hispanic Blacks (Charles 2003). At least since the Great Migration (beginning in the 1910s), furthermore, African Americans have been consistently excluded—often through deliberate legal and government-supported means—from a wide variety of housing opportunities, and disadvantaged geographically, economically, and socially through racially discriminatory housing processes (Rothstein 2017). Particularly in Chicago, a Black–White racial binary is embedded into the landscape. This geography informs the imaginary of the city for all residents, and as a result, a severe Black–White racial binary influences moving preferences and decisions.

Beyond Preferences, Discrimination, and Socioeconomic Disparities

This book contributes to a growing body of research that seeks to understand the complex processes that perpetuate racial segregation in the post–civil rights era. Most research on the causes of racial segregation has focused on three dominant theories: preferences, discrimination, and socioeconomic disparities, but recent research has suggested that viewing these theories as mutually exclusive and exhaustive competing theories obscures and minimizes the ways these mechanisms may interact (Krysan and Crowder 2017). Furthermore, while there is value in these dominant theories, they cannot fully explain how racial segregation has persisted at such high levels while progress has been made on racial attitudes, overt discrimination, and racial income disparities. The "big three theories" also do not cover ways that differences in the housing search process may effect outcomes (Crowder and Krysan 2016). New research in housing has highlighted the importance of studying this process and using findings from psychology to develop cognitively reasonable models to explain the process (Bruch and Feinberg 2017; Bruch, Hammond and Todd 2015; Bruch and Swait 2019; Krysan and Crowder 2017).

The first of the "big three," housing discrimination is known to be an important contributor to racial segregation, but we have reason to believe that it is not the only contributing factor. The 2012 Housing Discrimination Study conducted by the US Department of Housing and Urban Development showed that when Black homebuyers use the services of real-estate agents to aid in making a purchase, they receive quantitatively less information and are shown 17.7% fewer homes (Turner et al. 2013). Surprisingly, Scott South and Kyle Crowder found that levels of racial discrimination in housing markets as determined by audit studies are actually positively associated with Black mobility into Whiter areas, meaning that more discrimination occurs in places where more Black people are moving in. This finding suggests that while housing discrimination increases when more Black movers are interested in an area, it is often not fully effective in keeping Blacks from buying homes in an area. South and Crowder did not find evidence that discrimination hinders mobility into Whiter neighborhoods, but they did see that discrimination against African Americans was associated with Whites moving into Whiter neighborhoods. Of course, even if housing discrimination does not directly prevent African American households from moving into White neighborhoods, it can have many other adverse effects on Black households, including higher housing costs because the search process is made more onerous and choices are constrained (South and Crowder 1998).

In addition to discrimination, movers' preferences can affect racial segregation. Some have argued that preferences for living near kin or same-race neighbors may detract from more integrative moves, but Peter Rosenblatt and Stefanie Deluca (2012) found that poor African Americans using Moving to Opportunity housing choice vouchers never mentioned a preference for same-race neighbors and were as likely to state that they wanted to move away from friends and family as they were to state a desire to live near their family and friends. On the other hand, fear of racial hostility may dissuade some African Americans from moving into White neighborhoods (Krysan and Farley 2002). Another factor contributing to continued racial segregation of mobile individuals is that neighborhoods can change. Robert Sampson (2012) argues that neighborhoods can choose people, rather than the other way around. This phenomenon is evident when Black families move to integrated neighborhoods and White families leave, ultimately changing the demographics of the neighborhoods Black families chose. Furthermore, Whites continue to avoid areas with substantial numbers of Blacks (Bader and Krysan 2015; Quillian 2002) and have been shown to avoid areas near Black neighborhoods (Massey and Denton 1993). Finally, while some have suggested that neutral within-group racial attachment could explain these preferences, the evidence provides little support for this view. Camille Zubrinsky Charles (2003) found that neutral within-group attachment has little association preferences for same-race neighbors; instead, White people's negative attitudes towards other racial groups appear to drive their preferences, while fear of hostility from Whites affects the preferences of other groups. On a more hopeful note, Charles does find that all groups are willing to live in more racially integrated areas than they currently do, which suggests that preferences alone cannot explain the segregation that we see.

Much of what we know about the role of racial neighborhood composition preferences comes from neighborhood card studies, which have been highly valuable but abstract from actual housing decisions. These card studies were first introduced by Reynolds Farley, Howard Schuman, Suzanne Bianchi, Diane Colasanto, and Shirley Hatchett (1978) and were replicated several times thereafter (Farley, Fielding and Krysan 1997; Farley et al. 1993; Ihlanfeldt and Scafidi 2002). In neighborhood card studies, researchers present respondents with cards that depict neighborhoods with varying racial compositions graphically. Respondents then choose which neighborhoods they would be more or less willing to move into. We have learned valuable information from neighborhood card studies about what housing choices would be under these conditions. But the representation of housing choices in these studies is too static and simple to capture the full picture of housing decisions. Furthermore, because card studies measure preferences in an abstracted situation in which decisions are costless, these findings are unlikely to be as applicable to real-world situations as we would like.

Another way in which preferences matter is that homebuyers try to forecast the preferences of others when buying a home, because they are speculating on the future of the market to which their fortunes will be tied. More so than for Black people, because they are a larger group, White people's forecasts of other people's preferences can become self-fulfilling prophesies. So, while Whites and Blacks are engaged in the same housing game—trying to predict which neighborhoods will be more or less preferred by potential buyers in the years to come—White people have major structural advantage in playing.

Other researchers have looked to socioeconomic disparities between Blacks and Whites to explain racial segregation. While it is true that higher socioeconomic status African Americans tend to be less segregated from Whites than those of lower socioeconomic status, substantial differences persist between the neighborhoods where people of different racial and ethnic backgrounds but the same socioeconomic status live (Krysan and Crowder 2017). The simplest way to look at socioeconomic disparities is to examine income. For instance, Richard Alba, Logan and Stults (2000) looked at the effect of socioeconomic status on segregation for Black people in terms of income, education, and housing tenure. They found that middle-income Black people remain somewhat segregated from White people—while less so than poor Black people—and they still live in less advantaged neighborhoods than middle-income Whites. Another way of looking at socioeconomic disparities is wealth. Since the wealth gap between Black and White people is much larger than the income gap, researchers have long thought that differences in individual and parental wealth may explain differences in what neighborhoods Whites and Blacks move into. But Kyle Crowder, Scott South, and Erick Chavez (2006) found that wealth disparities alone explain only part of the differences between the neighborhoods that White and Black households move into.

To develop a better understanding of how racial segregation is created, this book explores processes of residential relocation and extends beyond simple explanations based on preferences, discrimination, and socioeconomic disparities. Specifically, I join researchers who are bringing in findings from psychology to develop cognitively plausible models of residential relocation decisions that take into account the heuristic nature of decision-making (Bruch and Feinberg 2017; Bruch, Hammond and Todd 2015; Krysan and Crowder 2017). By focusing on the homebuying process, this study provides both a subjective understanding of the decision-making process for African American aspiring homebuyers, and an analysis of how this subjectivity has implications for housing outcomes. Lower-middle-class African Americans are actively searching for stable and improving racially diverse neighborhoods—using reasonable strategies all the while—and sometimes even see themselves as being successful in these searches. But their strategies interact with structural constraints in ways that prevent their desired outcomes.

Foreclosure Crisis

I conducted the research for this book in the wake of the foreclosure crisis, during which African American homeowners were disadvantaged in new and especially painful ways. When Tiffany was first looking at the condo where I interviewed her in Bronzeville, the owner wanted her to buy it rather than rent it. Tiffany said the owner of the condo "purchased on the higher end of the market and she needs to sell it." At that time, though, Tiffany was not interested in buying a home. She explained: "I know how the market has recently crashed, a lot of people lost the equity in their home. I mean, I have relatives that lost a lot of money." Tiffany was well aware of the effects of the foreclosure crisis as she was living with the fallout all around her.

Tiffany's experience of being surrounded by people who lost big during the crisis is typical for African Americans. African American and Latino borrowers lost their homes at higher rates during the national foreclosure crisis than non-Hispanic White borrowers. In particular, high-income Black borrowers went into foreclosure disproportionately compared with non-Hispanic White borrowers. For example, Katrin Anacker, James Carr, and Archana Pradhan (2012) used the case of Prince George's County—a suburban county bordering Washington, D.C. and the highest-income, predominately Black county in the country—to investigate the causes of foreclosure for high-income African Americans. They found that exotic mortgages (including balloon mortgages, adjustable-rate mortgages, and high-cost mortgages) are responsible for these disproportionately high rates of foreclosure. Some of these problematic mortgages were given to high-income minority borrowers. Thus, these authors argue, it is not the case that overextended poor minorities drove the crisis. Rather, minorities of varying means were given mortgage loans with highly unfavorable terms.

During the mortgage crisis, the notion that loans had been given to minority borrowers who were less than creditworthy was frequently pointed to as a major cause of the crisis. Jacob Rugh and Douglas Massey (2010), however, found that foreclosure rates were not related to the expansion of borrowing to minority homeowners or the creditworthiness of borrowers. On the contrary, they assert that racial segregation was a major contributing cause to the crisis because this phenomenon enabled predatory subprime lending. Additionally, Matthew Hall, Kyle Crowder, and Amy Spring (2015) found that the foreclosure crisis increased average Black–White segregation across US metropolitan areas. Both majority-minority and integrated neighborhoods had higher rates of foreclosures than predominately White neighborhoods. Furthermore, higher rates of foreclosure were associated with larger White population loss and greater increases in Black and

Hispanic populations. In other words, integrated neighborhoods often had high rates of foreclosure and this led to increased levels of White flight.

This book demonstrates how foreclosures wrought more than just financial havoc on otherwise possibly upwardly mobile African American families. Popular media used these high rates of foreclosure among African Americans and Latinos to stigmatize and scapegoat these groups for the financial crisis (Squires 2008). I argue that since African Americans are generally strong adherents to the ideology of the American Dream, many of the foreclosed upon felt this moral cost personally. Furthermore, African Americans who were foreclosed upon experienced both the trauma of losing their homes and racial stigma from this myth of irresponsibility.

The foreclosure crisis has created a heightened sense of awareness of the potential pitfalls of homeownership, especially for African Americans. Despite the particular challenges facing African American homebuyers, many remain committed to this goal because of the moral value attached to the status of homeowner. For this reason, many African Americans remain cautiously optimistic about the possibility of buying a house, and they still see it as an important goal. In addition to the perceived financial benefits of homeownership, middle-income African American homebuyers value homeownership as a marker of adulthood, for the greater control over living space that it provides, as well as evidence of achieving the American Dream. Finally, I found that working-class African American homebuyers believe that the responsibilities of homeownership help to shape homeowners as citizens and community members.

The Study

The homebuyers in this study are best characterized as working-class, but they hold decidedly middle-class aspirations. They are motivated by a desire for the comforts of a bourgeois home, the status of middle-class respectability and the responsibilities that come with this lifestyle. They form an interesting group because they are at a critical moment in their process of solidifying their middle-class status by investing in their own home. They are also an understudied population. This group is doing better than the low-income subsidized renters studied in work on the Moving to Opportunity experiment (Goering and Feins 2003; Rosenblatt and DeLuca 2012), but not as well as the upper-middle-class Black families studied by Karyn Lacy (2007) in her ethnography of Washington, D.C. area suburbs. Generally, the homebuyers in this study are much less likely to have experienced living in predominately White areas. In turn, when they are considering predominately White areas, those areas do not look like the affluent suburb of Fairfax County that Lacy studied. Instead, these neighborhoods are more similar to the defensive White working-class neighborhood in Maria Kefalas's *Working-Class Heroes: Protecting Home, Community, and Nation in a Chicago Neighborhood* (2003). The homebuyers in this study are the African American equivalent to this struggling working-class.

They hold very similar values and ideologies about home upkeep and meticulous lawn care. Ironically, they are also precisely the people whom the White working class fear.

For this study, I conducted qualitative interviews with sixty-eight African American aspiring homebuyers (from sixty-five separate households)[1] looking to buy a home in the Chicago metropolitan area to investigate the housing-search process and residential relocation decisions in the context of a racially segregated metropolitan region.

I recruited these homebuyers from homebuyer education classes and followed them throughout their process of searching for and buying a home. Three homebuyer education classes were selected to include a predominately Black urban area (Roseland, 14 respondents), a racially transitioning suburban area (East Hazel Crest, 40), and a stably integrated suburban area (Oak Park, 14). Still, attendees at these sites were often looking for homes in other parts of the metropolitan region as well. I provide more details on the recruitment process and the interviews in the methodological appendix. The homebuyers were mostly working- or lower-middle-class (61% of these homebuyers had annual household incomes between $25,000 and $75,000). For their highest level of education, 35% of the homebuyers had attained some college and 52% had attained a college degree or higher.

Most of the participants in the study were female (78%). This gender mix is partially because some of the households were female-headed; in cases where the household was headed by a heterosexual couple and only one person participated in the study, it was usually the woman. It appeared that women were often taking the lead organizing role in their family's homebuying process. Others have found that, because African American women have a long legacy of working outside the home, cultural scripts for ideal middle-class family life are distinct for this group. For African Americans, the ideal mother and wife is expected to be successful in work outside the home (Dow 2019). My research suggests that this cultural ideal may translate to African American women taking more of a leadership role in the homebuying process. In the book *Race for Profit: How Banks and the Real Estate Industry Undermined Black Homeownership*, Keeanga-Yamahtta Taylor (2019) explains how new housing policies in the 1970s targeted African American women (who were more likely to be heads of households than White women) for what she terms predatory inclusion in the housing market. Relatedly, Matthew Desmond (2016) argues the racially biased and predatory low-income rental market exploits and impoverishes Black women. The fact that Black women are more often heads of households means that they are exposed to more of the harms caused by racially unjust home ownership and rental markets.

Initially, 42% of the homebuyers lived in suburbs, and the remainder lived in the city of Chicago. I was able to follow sixteen homebuyers through to their move to a new home. Of the sixteen who moved to new homes, nine moved to suburbs of Chicago. I specifically focus on the homebuying process in a large metropolitan region because African American suburbanization has accelerated in recent decades across the United States (Frey 2011; Wiese 2004). The number of African Americans who moved to the suburbs between 1960 and 2000 is larger than the number who moved during the Great Migration, a period that lasted nearly twice as long, from 1910 to 1970 (Wiese 2004). In 2010, census data showed that for the first time ever, in the 100 largest US metropolitan areas, a majority of African Americans live in the suburbs. At the same time, the largest southern metropolitan areas have growing African American populations, and African Americans in all regions are tending to move to the suburbs (Sullivan 2011). While the suburbs have been associated with Whiteness, and have been a site for constructing White racial identity (Gans 1982), they have long been more racially diverse than is commonly understood, and they are now home to the majority of racial minorities and immigrants (Lung-Amam 2017). In light of these recent demographic shifts, a metropolitan perspective is necessary to understand the dynamics of racially segregated housing.

Furthermore, African American suburbanization has not necessarily brought about greater racial integration. Overall, Black–White segregation is declining slowly in the United States, but those declines are uneven and segregation remains high. One way to quantify the persistence of segregation is the dissimilarity index, which indicates the percentage of either group who would need to relocate in order to achieve an even geographic distribution of groups. By 2010, the average Black–White dissimilarity index had decreased to 60, from 78 in 1970. A dissimilarity rate of 60 means that 60% of the Black or White population would need to move for an even geographic distribution of these groups (Rugh and Massey 2014). Similarly, Massey and Denton (1989) developed the term hypersegregation to describe how Blacks are highly segregated on multiple geographic dimensions in many US metropolitan areas, resulting in a more extreme type of segregation than that experienced by other racial and ethnic groups. Segregation has declined more slowly in areas characterized by hypersegregation (Rugh and Massey 2014). Finally, the persistence of segregation does not reflect the preferences of most African Americans who tend to prefer racially integrated neighborhoods (Krysan and Farley 2002). Despite the preferences of African Americans for integrated neighborhoods and the trend of African American suburbanization, Black–White racial segregation remains at high levels.

Racial segregation has largely persisted in the suburbs (Charles 2003; Lake 1981). Robert Lake studied the unprecedented growth of African American suburbanization in the 1970s and found that African Americans were moving to suburbs that already had large numbers of African Americans and were experiencing White flight. He showed that the process of Black in-migration and White flight extended from highly segregated central cities into the suburbs during the 1970s and led to a replication of racial segregation throughout metropolitan areas (Lake 1981). Researchers have shown that White flight has persisted in the suburbs, and through 2010 was more common in middle-class suburbs than in poor suburbs (Kye 2018). On the other hand, there has been some growth in the rate of African Americans moving to areas that are not predominately Black or contiguous with predominately Black areas. Within the Chicago metropolitan region, both predominately Black suburbs of Chicago and some suburbs with very small Black populations experienced African American in-migration during the 2000s (Trotter 2011). This suggests some potential for an increase in the number of racially integrated Black–White communities. Because of a wide variety of suburbs with varying racial compositions, the Chicago metropolitan area is an ideal case for comparing the experiences of households moving to suburbs with distinct racial compositions.

In terms of the setting, it is important to note that Chicago is an extreme case for studying racial segregation. As of 2010, in the Chicago-Joliet-Naperville Metropolitan Area, 76% of the Black or White population would need to move in order to achieve an even geographic distribution of groups. Using the dissimilarity index, the Chicago metropolitan area is the sixth most-segregated in the United States. Furthermore, the dissimilarity index does not take into account the level of overall diversity, which could be viewed as the potential an area has for more integrated neighborhoods. Nate Silver (2015) developed an integration-segregation index which quantifies the relationship between citywide and neighborhood diversity scores; by this metric, the most segregated cities are diverse in terms of the overall population but have little diversity within their neighborhoods. Using this metric and data from the 2010 census, he found that of the largest 100 cities, Chicago was the most segregated.

While Chicago has an extreme level of racial segregation, areas with large Black populations tend to have high levels of Black–White segregation, so many African Americans live in this type of environment. As of 2010, African Americans were hypersegregated in twenty-one metropolitan areas, including Chicago. Across the United States, 33% of all African Americans lived in these hypersegregated metropolitan areas, and another 21% lived in highly segregated metropolitan areas (Massey 2015). Chicago was one of eight metropolitan areas with a high score on all five of the geographic dimensions used to determine hypersegregation. More broadly, six of these eight most-hypersegregated metropolitan areas are in the Midwest (Massey and Tannen 2015). Therefore, while Chicago is an extreme case of racial segregation, it can be considered representative of the type of place where more than half of the African American population resides.

Chicago is also emblematic of the trend towards African American suburbanization. By using the Chicago metropolitan area as a case study, I am able to examine dynamics of racial segregation and residential relocation across city neighborhoods and suburbs. Between 2000 and 2010, the population of the city of Chicago shrank by 200,418 people. Of those 200,418 lost residents, 178,126 were African American. While Cook County also lost African Americans overall, a number of suburban towns within Cook County simultaneously had large gains in their African American populations (Mackun et al. 2011; Trotter 2011). All of the "collar counties" experienced an increase in their African American population (US Census Bureau 2000, 2010), suggesting an increase in African Americans moving to far-flung suburbs or exurbs. While Chicago's experience appears to be indicative of some national trends, including the increased suburbanization of African Americans and reverse migration to the South, this loss of population is an extreme case (Holloway 2011). Among the ten US cities with the largest African American populations, Chicago had the second-largest percentage decrease in this demographic, behind only Detroit (Zotti 2012). The trend of African American suburbanization has been accelerating in Chicago and other northern industrial cities since the 1980s (Wiese 2004), but 2000–2010 was the first decade when African Americans made up a majority of the population decrease in Chicago. These trends make the Chicago metropolitan region a compelling site to investigate African American suburbanization.

From one perspective, this decline in African American population in Chicago may simply indicate that African Americans are in a better financial position to act on their preferences for suburban residence. It could be the case that suburbanization results in African Americans accessing stable suburban locations that match their preferences, provide access to more resources, and allow for comparable wealth accumulation as Whites. The reality is that Chicago's suburbs vary greatly in terms of neighborhood contexts. It is not always the case that geographic residential mobility from the suburb to the city results in upward contextual mobility. Since White flight has touched many of Chicago's suburbs, the problems of racially discriminatory housing markets have plagued these areas. The variation in racial demographics between Chicago's suburbs allows for a study that covers many different possible trajectories of residential relocation. For homebuyers, these varying trajectories are particularly important because they tie directly to the process of wealth formation.

The Racial Map of Chicagoland

The city of Chicago and the vast sprawling suburbs that surround it are sometimes collectively called Chicagoland. The city sits on Lake Michigan, with a downtown area called the Loop at its center, named for shape created by the elevated train lines. Neighborhoods with distinct characters, histories, ethnic and racial makeups, and socioeconomic statuses radiate out from the Loop to the north, west, and south (with the lake to the east). From there, seemingly endless suburbs ring the city. These suburbs may seem very similar to one another on the surface. For starters, the names tend to be incredibly generic and indistinguishable. The Chicago suburbs seemingly could have been named by randomly generating nature nouns, with each suburb arbitrarily given two. There is a Lake Forest, a Crystal Lake, an Oak Park, a Park Forest, and a Forest Park. And some aspects of their suburban landscapes are quite similar—most are comprised of many single-family detached homes, strip-mall style shopping centers, and shopping malls. On the other hand, these suburbs vary greatly in the prices of the homes, economic resources available for funding important services, retail options, and their socioeconomic, ethnic, and racial makeups. For instance, Lake Forest, a northern suburb located on Lake Michigan, is 1% non-Hispanic Black, while Park Forest, to the south of the city, is 59% non-Hispanic Black (US Census Bureau 2010).

Tiffany's neighborhood of Bronzeville occupies a very particular place in Chicago's complex racial map. Bronzeville is located at the core of Chicago's historic Black Belt. The Black Belt has expanded greatly over time, no longer resembling a belt, but a large band across the western suburbs, parts of the West Side of the city, the South Side, and the South suburbs (sometimes called the Southland). Within this large band are many highly varied neighborhoods that range widely in terms of their housing stock, retail and business composition, racial makeup, and socioeconomic demographics. Within the South and West Sides of the city are poor, nearly all-Black neighborhoods with mixes of high-rise rentals and single-family homes, and there are more economically mixed, primarily Black areas with more middle-class households, like Bronzeville. Some central areas like Bronzeville have more condo buildings and walk-ups. The outer ring of the city, sometimes called the Bungalow Belt, has more single-family homes, and these neighborhoods have a variety of racial and socioeconomic compositions. In many ways, the Bungalow neighborhoods of the city look much like the inner ring suburbs that surround them. To the south and west of Chicago there are a number of older suburbs, like Riverdale, that are currently experiencing a racial transition as they shift from being predominately White to predominately Black. Meanwhile, the northern suburbs, especially those to the east, along the lake, remain largely White. There are just a few stably integrated neighborhoods scattered throughout this band, including Oak Park in the western suburbs and Beverly in the Bungalow Belt.

This racial map affects not just where people live but also where they work, go to school, meet up with friends, what they find familiar, and what feels far away. Disparate opportunities for jobs, schools, and financial investment in housing are available to people depending on their location on this map. Of course, when looking at individual decisions about where to live, we could emphasize that these are personal decisions and therefore of little relevance to the public. No one directly forced the homebuyers in this study to buy in a particular neighborhood. Today, we do not see the kind of overt *de jure* segregation that had created neighborhoods like Bronzeville in the first place. Ultimately, though, social processes do push Black homebuyers to buy in places that are less racially diverse and less economically stable than they desire. Broader social structures work against these neighborhoods and loosen Black homebuyers' foothold in the middle class, and make their access to the American Dream more precarious.

Outline of the Book

The structure of the book roughly follows the homebuying process. In Chapters 2 and 3 I explain the motivations for homeownership among this population. For

African Americans, homeownership represents two major strains of the American Dream. Typically, in the American Dream of homeownership, the home represents freedom and success. While this is true for Americans in general, for African Americans in particular, homeownership also represents achievement in terms of the American Dream of equality. For White Americans, these ideals of individual success and social equality can be in tension with each other, but for African Americans, the concepts are deeply intertwined and both are symbolized by homeownership. Because homeownership is seen as an essential piece of successful middle-class adulthood, moreover, it is perceived to be an important life-stage milestone for African Americans, despite—or even because of—the fact that they typically buy homes later than Whites. Both the American Dream and the delay in homeownership shape what kinds of homes middle-income African Americans are looking to invest in. In the remaining chapters, I explore how African American homebuyers try to overcome these structural obstacles. In Chapter 4 I explain the housing search strategies employed by homebuyers in pursuit of this dream. In Chapter 5 I address the ways in which existing assistance programs shape the search process. And in Chapter 6 I describe the kinds of places that homebuyers ultimately moved to and what obstacles kept many aspiring homebuyers from achieving their dreams. In the conclusion, I synthesize findings from observing the home-buying process for middle-income African Americans and suggest potential policy interventions.

Tiffany did not buy her home during the course of this study, but she hoped to do so in the future. When I asked if she thought owning a home would change anything about her life, she said, "I hope so"—indeed, she thought it wouldn't just change her life, it would change *her*. She thought owning a home would help her become better at saving and generally demonstrate her sense of responsibility and ability to commit. When she spoke of homeowners in general, she talked about how much they help bolster neighborhoods because they invest in the appearance of their own space and the community. Despite all the warning signs she saw in her own family experience and in her Bronzeville neighborhood, she held out hope that she would one day take on this transformative status of homeowner.

And for the prospective homebuyers who were successful, it felt like a dream come true, albeit one that was fleeting, not firmly grasped. After purchasing her home in the suburb of Lynwood, Kaya proclaimed, "I'm so excited. It's like a dream home. I mean, it has everything I want in it." At the same time, Kaya ended up compromising on some aspects of the purchase that were very important to her. In our first interview she said she wanted to buy a house in a racially "mixed community" with "good schools." In Lynwood, she felt that "schools in the area" were "not as good" as she would have liked and that "it's not necessarily a mixed area [...] because I haven't seen a lot of other ethnicities besides mine." In the following chapters, I explain why homebuyers like Kaya can feel successful in achieving the dream in some sense, but ambivalent about the ways in which the areas where they end up fall short of their ideal. Ultimately, working-class African Americans keep grasping for their own version of the American Dream even when success comes at a higher price with greater precarity.

Note

1 I refer to the individual homebuyers by pseudonyms throughout the book.

References

Alba, Richard D., John R. Logan, and Brian J. Stults. 2000. "How Segregated Are Middle-Class African Americans?" *Social Problems* 47(4): 543–558. https://doi.org/10.2307/3097134.

Anacker, Katrin B., James H. Carr, and Archana Pradhan. 2012. "Analyzing Foreclosures Among High-Income Black/African American and Hispanic/Latino Borrowers in Prince George's County, Maryland." *Housing and Society* 39(1): 1–28. https://doi.org/10.1080/08882746.2012.11430598.

Bader, Michael D. M., and Maria Krysan. 2015. "Community Attraction and Avoidance in Chicago: What's Race Got to Do with It?" *The Annals of the American Academy of Political and Social Science* 660(1): 261–281. https://doi.org/10.1177/0002716215577615.

Baldwin, Davarian L. 2007. *Chicago's New Negroes: Modernity, the Great Migration, and Black Urban Life*. Chapel Hill: University of North Carolina Press.

Brooks, Gwendolyn. 1951. "They Call it Bronzeville." Holiday (October 1951): 60–64, 67, 112–116.

Bruch, Elizabeth, and Fred Feinberg. 2017. "Decision-Making Processes in Social Contexts." *Annual Review of Sociology* 43(1): 207–227. https://doi.org/10.1146/annurev-soc-060116-053622.

Bruch, Elizabeth, and Joffre Swait. 2019. "Choice Set Formation in Residential Mobility and Its Implications for Segregation Dynamics." *Demography* 56(5): 1665–1692. https://doi.org/10.1007/s13524-019-00810-5.

Bruch, Elizabeth, Ross A. Hammond, and Peter M. Todd. 2015. "Coevolution of Decision-Making and Social Environments." In *Emerging Trends in the Social and Behavioral Sciences*, edited by R. A. Scott, S. M. Kosslyn, and M. Buchmann. New York: John Wiley & Sons.

Charles, Camille Zubrinsky. 2003. "The Dynamics of Racial Residential Segregation." *Annual Review of Sociology* 29: 167–207. www.jstor.org/stable/30036965.

———. 2006. *Won't You Be My Neighbor: Race, Class, and Residence in Los Angeles*. New York: Russell Sage Foundation.

Clergé, Orly. 2019. *The New Noir: Race, Identity, and Diaspora in Black Suburbia*. Berkeley: University of California Press.

Crowder, Kyle, and Maria Krysan. 2016. "Moving Beyond the Big Three: A Call for New Approaches to Studying Racial Residential Segregation." *City & Community* 15(1): 18–22. https://doi.org/10.1111/cico.12148.

Crowder, Kyle, Scott J. South, and Erick Chavez. 2006. "Wealth, Race, and Inter-Neighborhood Migration." *American Sociological Review* 71(1): 72–94. https://doi.org/10.1177/000312240607100104.

Desmond, Matthew. 2016. *Evicted: Poverty and Profit in the American City*. New York: Broadway Books.

Dow, Dawn Marie. 2019. *Mothering While Black: Boundaries and Burdens of Middle-Class Parenthood*. Berkeley: University of California Press.

Farley, Reynolds, Charlotte Steeh, Tara Jackson, Maria Krysan, and Keith Reeves. 1993. "Continued Racial Residential Segregation in Detroit: 'Chocolate City, Vanilla Suburbs' Revisited." *Journal of Housing Research* 4(1): 1–38. www.jstor.org/stable/24832753.

Farley, Reynolds, Elaine L Fielding, and Maria Krysan. 1997. "The Residential Preferences of Blacks and Whites: A Four-Metropolis Analysis." *Housing Policy Debate* 8(4): 763–800. https://doi.org/10.1080/10511482.1997.9521278.

Farley, Reynolds, Howard Schuman, Suzanne Bianchi, Diane Colasanto, and Shirley Hatchett. 1978. "'Chocolate City, Vanilla Suburbs': Will the Trend toward Racially Separate Communities Continue?" *Social Science Research* 7(4): 319–344. https://doi.org/10.1016/0049-089X(78)90017-0.

Frey, William H. 2011. "Melting Pot Cities and Suburbs: Racial and Ethnic Change in Metro America in the 2000s." Washington, D.C.: Metropolitan Policy Program, Brookings Institute.

Gans, Herbert J. 1982. *The Levittowners: Ways of Life and Politics in a New Suburban Community*, 2nd ed. New York: Columbia University Press.

Goering, John M., and Judith D. Feins. 2003. *Choosing a Better Life?: Evaluating the Moving to Opportunity Social Experiment*. Washington, D.C.: The Urban Institute.

Goodman, Laurie, Jun Zhu, and Rolf Pendall. 2017. "Are Gains in Black Homeownership History?" Urban Wire: Housing and Housing Finance. www.urban.org/urban-wire/are-gains-black-homeownership-history.

Hall, Matthew, Kyle Crowder, and Amy Spring. 2015. "Neighborhood Foreclosures, Racial/Ethnic Transitions, and Residential Segregation." *American Sociological Review* 80(3): 526–549. https://doi.org/10.1177/0003122415581334.

Holloway, Lynette 2011. "Chicago's Shrinking Black Community." The Root. www.theroot.com/chicagos-shrinking-black-community-1790865474.

Ifill, Sherrilyn. 2019. "Focus on the Costs of Segregation for All." in *The Dream Revisited: Contemporary Debates about Housing, Segregation, and Opportunity*, edited by I. Ellen and J. Steil. New York: Columbia University Press.

Ihlanfeldt, Keith R., and Benjamin Scafidi. 2002. "Black Self-Segregation as a Cause of Housing Segregation: Evidence from the Multi-City Study of Urban Inequality." *Journal of Urban Economics* 51(2): 366–390. https://doi.org/10.1006/juec.2001.2249.

Kefalas, Maria. 2003. *Working-Class Heroes: Protecting Home, Community, and Nation in a Chicago Neighborhood*. Berkeley: University of California Press.

Krysan, Maria, and Kyle Crowder. 2017. *Cycle of Segregation: Social Processes and Residential Stratification*. New York: Russell Sage Foundation.

Krysan, Maria, and Reynolds Farley. 2002. "The Residential Preferences of Blacks: Do They Explain Persistent Segregation?" *Social Forces* 80(3): 937–980. https://www.jstor.org/stable/3086462.

Kye, Samuel H. 2018. "The Persistence of White Flight in Middle-Class Suburbia." *Social Science Research* 72: 38–52. https://doi.org/10.1016/j.ssresearch.2018.02.005.

Lacy, Karyn. 2007. *Blue-Chip Black: Race, Class, and Status in the New Black Middle Class*. Berkeley: University of California Press.

Lake, Robert W. 1981. *The New Suburbanites: Race and Housing in the Suburbs*. New York: Routledge.

Lung-Amam, Willow. 2017. *Trespassers? Asian Americans and the Battle for Suburbia*. Berkeley: University of California Press.

Mackun, Paul J., Steven Wilson, Thomas R. Fischetti, and Justyna Goworowska. 2011. "Population Distribution and Change: 2000 to 2010." Washington, D.C.: US Census Bureau.

Massey, Douglas S. 2015. "The Legacy of the 1968 Fair Housing Act." *Sociological Forum* 30(S1): 571–588. https://doi.org/10.1111/socf.12178.

Massey, Douglas S., and Nancy A. Denton. 1989. "Hypersegregation in US Metropolitan Areas: Black and Hispanic Segregation along Five Dimensions." *Demography* 26(3): 373–391. https://doi.org/10.2307/2061599.

———. 1993. *American Apartheid: Segregation and the Making of the Underclass.* Cambridge: Harvard University Press.

Massey, Douglas S., and Jonathan Tannen. 2015. "A Research Note on Trends in Black Hypersegregation." *Demography* 52(3): 1025–1034. https://doi.org/10.1007/s13524-015-0381-6.

Pattillo, Mary. 2019. "The Problem of Integration." In *The Dream Revisited: Contemporary Debates About Housing, Segregation, and Opportunity*, edited by I. Ellen and J. Steil. New York: Columbia University Press.

Quillian, Lincoln. 2002. "Why is Black–White Residential Segregation So Persistent?: Evidence on Three Theories from Migration Data." *Social Science Research* 31(2): 197–229. https://doi.org/10.1006/ssre.2001.0726.

Rosenblatt, Peter, and Stefanie DeLuca. 2012. "'We Don't Live Outside, We Live in Here': Neighborhood and Residential Mobility Decisions among Low-Income Families." *City & Community* 11(3): 254–284. https://doi.org/10.1111/j.1540-6040.2012.01413.x.

Rothstein, Richard. 2017. *The Color of Law: A Forgotten History of How Our Government Segregated America.* New York: Liveright Publishing Corporation.

Rugh, Jacob S., and Douglas S. Massey. 2010. "Racial Segregation and the American Foreclosure Crisis." *American Sociological Review* 75(5): 629–651. https://www.jstor.org/stable/20799483.

———. 2014. "Segregation in Post–Civil Rights America: Stalled Integration or End of the Segregated Century?" *Du Bois Review: Social Science Research on Race* 11(2): 205–232. https://doi.org/10.1017/S1742058X13000180.

Sampson, Robert J. 2012. *Great American City: Chicago and the Enduring Neighborhood Effect.* Chicago: The University of Chicago Press.

Satter, Beryl. 2009. *Family Properties: Race, Real Estate, and the Exploitation of Black Urban America.* New York: Metropolitan Books.

Schlabach, Elizabeth Schroeder. 2012. *Along the Streets of Bronzeville: Black Chicago's Literary Landscape.* Champaign, IL: University of Illinois Press.

Shapiro, Thomas M. 2004. *The Hidden Cost of Being African American: How Wealth Perpetuates Inequality.* New York: Oxford University Press.

Sharkey, Patrick. 2013. *Stuck in Place: Urban Neighborhoods and the End of Progress Toward Racial Equality.* Chicago: University of Chicago Press.

Silver, Nate. 2015. "The Most Diverse Cities Are Often the Most Segregated." FiveThirty Eight. https://fivethirtyeight.com/features/the-most-diverse-cities-are-often-the-most-segregated/

South, Scott J., and Kyle D. Crowder. 1998. "Housing Discrimination and Residential Mobility: Impacts for Blacks and Whites." *Population Research and Policy Review* 17(4): 369–387. www.jstor.org/stable/40230196.

Soyer, Michaela. 2016. *A Dream Denied: Incarceration, Recidivism, and Young Minority Men in America.* Berkeley: University of California Press.

Squires, Gregory D. 2008. "Scapegoating Blacks for the Economic Crisis." *Poverty and Race* 17(6): 3–4. www.prrac.org/newsletters/novdec2008.pdf.

Sullivan, John. 2011. "African Americans Moving South—and to the Suburbs." *Race, Poverty and the Environment* 18(2): 16–19. www.reimaginerpe.org/files/18-2.sullivan.pdf.

Sullivan, Laura, Tatjana Meschede, Lars Dietrich, Thomas Shapiro, Amy Traub, Catherine Ruetschlin and Tamara Draut. 2015. "The Racial Wealth Gap: Why Policy Matters." New York: Institute on Assets and Social Policy, Brandeis University.

Taylor, Keeanga-Yamahtta. 2019. *Race for Profit: How Banks and the Real Estate Industry Undermined Black Homeownership*. Chapel Hill: University of North Carolina Press.

Trotter, Joanna. 2011. "2010 Census: African-Americans Leaving City for Suburbs." Metropolitan Planning Council. www.metroplanning.org/news/6140/2010-Census-African-Americans-leaving-city-for-suburbs.

Turner, Margery Austin, Rob Santos, Diane K. Levy, Doug Wissoker, Claudia L. Aranda, and Rob Pitingolo. 2013. "Housing Discrimination Against Racial and Ethnic Minorities 2012." Washington, D.C.: Office of Policy Development and Research.

US Census Bureau. 1990. "Census 1990." Social Explorer Tables. US Census Bureau and Social Explorer.

———. 2000. "Census 2000." Social Explorer Tables. US Census Bureau and Social Explorer.

———. 2010. "Census 2010." Social Explorer Tables. US Census Bureau and Social Explorer.

Wiese, Andrew. 2004. *Places of Their Own: African American Suburbanization in the Twentieth Century*. Chicago: University of Chicago Press.

Zotti, Ed. 2012. "Where Everybody Went." Straight Dope Chicago, Chicago Reader. https://web.archive.org/web/20120527090737/http://chicago.straightdope.com/sdccensus1.php

2

THE AFRICAN AMERICAN DREAM OF HOMEOWNERSHIP

I met with Barbara in a rental apartment in the quiet suburb of La Grange, Illinois. She shares the apartment with her adult daughter, teenage granddaughter, and her friendly dog who spent most of our interview lazing under the dining room table. Barbara told me about how she had owned a few homes in the past:

> I owned a condo, too. I had rented it out and then owned a two-flat unit, two units; and then I sold the condo, lived in the two unit, and then I was forced to sell it because of hardship. My mom died, so that was an income that was gone. And then you have to get people out of the building because they ain't paying rent and all that, so I used up all my resources. And so I just wanted to get away from up under it, so I did a short sale, and so then I moved to Berwyn, in those two locations, and then I moved out here. And I think I've been out here almost ten years, right? [She asked her daughter who was sitting across the kitchen table] Close. It's been close to ten years since I—and I almost fainted when I found out I had lived here that long, because we was used to living—we used to live as children, we lived in homes from Florida. I lived in a home with my mother and her husband, then I moved to my grandparents—they had a home—so here we are, back to trying to get back into the American Dream.

For Barbara, losing her home represents a fall from grace under the terms of the American Dream. That Barbara uses the word "home" exclusively to mean an owner-occupied house demonstrates the importance of owner status to her. To note, using the term "home" in this way was common among the homebuyers I interviewed. Barbara buys into the underlying promise of the American Dream—if you work hard and live responsibly, you can own a house. Despite ten years in rental housing as a result of losing her home, she is convinced that this is a detour from her American Dream. She is frustrated by her inability to maintain the trappings of the American Dream that her parents and grandparents had. For homebuyers like Barbara, success in homeownership is the basis for a personal identity as a responsible moral citizen. This success also means continuing a legacy of upward mobility over the course of generations. By this same logic, the stalling of that progress can be felt as a deeply personal loss for reasons that go far beyond the financial consequences.

The financial aspects of homeownership are interwoven with emotional aspects of this undertaking. For instance, I interviewed another homebuyer, Sarah, in her bungalow on the South Side of the city, which was in foreclosure at the time. Sarah explained that due to rising monthly rates she could not keep up with her adjustable-rate mortgage:

> First, they said it was going to go up every six months, then after that it seems like it's every month. Every month I get a bill, the rate just keep going higher and higher. I'm like, who could afford that?

Her monthly payments started at $735 and soon rose to $1,700. At the same time that the payments increased, Sarah divorced her husband, who was no longer helping with the payments. The combination of the change in her family situation and the ballooning mortgage payments made it impossible for Sarah to continue to pay. Even for aspiring homebuyers who did not have personal experiences with a terrible mortgage arrangement, the homebuyer education classes were peppered with similar horror stories. Generally, this population of homebuyers was highly aware of and concerned about the possibility of foreclosure.

Even with direct experience with foreclosure, homebuyers remained deeply invested in the goal of homeownership. Sarah wants desperately to buy a new home despite this traumatic experience with homeownership. She mentioned that she has two large dogs, so it would be hard to find a rental property where she could bring them. She also declared, "I really don't want to rent no more—period—anyway. I really want my own. I want something in my own name, something [of] my own. That it's like a legacy."

When I called her a few months later, Sarah was still living in the foreclosed house, but she had received a notice the day prior saying that she needed to leave immediately. That weekend, Sarah was planning to move to her brother's house for a few weeks. She also spoke to a loan officer and determined that she could get another mortgage with a cosigner, and her son offered to cosign the loan for a new home. Sarah was determined not to be a renter, even for a short period of time.

Many of the African American homebuyers interviewed for this study have had some experience with foreclosure. Seven homebuyers had a first-hand experience with foreclosure, including losing a home to foreclosure, losing a home because they could no longer pay their mortgage but avoiding an actual foreclosure, being forced to leave a rental unit because their landlord went into foreclosure, or living in a home owned by a family member who lost it to foreclosure. Many others had seen multiple foreclosures in the neighborhoods where they lived. Experience with foreclosure had led some respondents to be more wary of certain aspects of the homebuying process. Since I had recruited participants from homebuyer education classes, my sample was highly likely to include many people who were still strongly committed to the goal of homeownership despite challenges. To investigate this homebuying group further, the research question became simply: why are these individuals pursuing homeownership? This group remained committed to homeownership, in part, because of the moral status attached to achieving this goal.

Finally, the foreclosure crisis had grave effects on many of the neighborhoods where these aspiring homebuyers lived. Sarah told me about the effect that other foreclosures have had on her neighborhood:

> You could drive around and you could see them empty for five, six, seven years, and people who was on drugs just come and clean it out, take everything out. If the original people was in there, they would have kept that up going, they wouldn't have to be messing up the windows, burning houses down.

Foreclosures made it difficult to maintain the outward appearance of the neighborhood and social cohesion. Foreclosure is a deep personal wound for the homeowner who experiences it and a blight on the whole surrounding community.

For African American homebuyers, success at the American Dream of homeownership is directly related to the dream of equality for African Americans. As these aspiring homebuyers fall behind compared to their parents and grandparents, their struggle raises doubts about the degree to which African Americans can have a reasonable expectation of success in this most widely recognized form of the American Dream. In this chapter, I argue that the fallout from the foreclosure crisis is particularly painful because it creates holes in two important aspects of the American Dream for African Americans: the dream of homeownership, and the dream of equality. The foreclosure crisis has done irreparable damage to both of these dreams on an individual basis and in terms of the collective experience of neighborhoods.

What Does the American Dream Mean for African Americans?

I did not begin this project thinking that the American Dream would be so central, but it quickly became evident that the idea of the dream is still central to how homebuyers think about the meaning of owning a home. At the homebuyer education classes where I recruited participants, each homebuyer received a manual, "Realizing the American Dream," and homebuyers frequently use the term "American Dream" themselves—without any prompting—when describing their reasons for pursuing homeownership.

The homebuyers in this study were motivated to buy because of their deep belief in the American Dream, but what exactly did the American Dream mean to them? In his work on the historical development of aspects of the American Dream, Jim Cullen (2004) argues that homeownership is how the largest number of Americans have experienced the achievement of the American Dream in concrete terms. He claims that the American Dream of homeownership has the broadest appeal and is the most widely realized of any version of this ideology. Historically, this version of the dream has its roots in the Jeffersonian ideal of a republic of independent farmers. The American ideal of freedom rests on the ability of individual citizens to be the masters of their own lives, pursuing their own goals in their own space.

Cullen (2004) also points to another aspect of the American Dream, which is the dream of equality. In order for the ideology of the American Dream to remain salient, people must believe it to be equitable. There has long been a notion in American politics that equality and freedom are in dialectical tension, but both freedom and equality are equally salient for African Americans who have historically been at the center of political struggles around these two ideals. Arguably, the notion that these ideals are in tension comes from the perspective of Whites, while the ideals are deeply intertwined for African Americans. Furthermore, Charles Willie and Richard Reddick (2010) argue that middle-class African Americans prioritize the value of hard work and diligence—associated with the American Dream—as both individually beneficial and important for the racial group. Personal success can be an opportunity to challenge racial stereotypes and create opportunities for other members of the group. Thus, for African American homebuyers, success indicates moral status for themselves and for the group. In sum, homeownership is infused with a particular moral significance for African Americans.

The ideology of the American Dream also rests on the romanticized idea that no matter the societal obstacles, with hard work one can overcome them and achieve success. This dream obscures fundamental realties about inequality and barriers to opportunity in American society. Heather Beth Johnson (2015) found that the emphasis on meritocracy in the American Dream leads wealthy families to keep their wealth hidden and private, obscuring the role of that wealth in creating inequalities. Ultimately, this leaves less wealthy people unaware of the greater challenges that they face, and even to blame themselves for their inability to achieve homeownership as opposed to critiquing larger structures of inequality. Michaela Soyer (2016) conceptualizes the American Dream as a belief that an individual can exercise agency to overcome structural barriers. This belief distracts from the reality of pervasive social barriers and inequality of opportunity inherent in society. She found that overly optimistic perceptions of agency did not help juvenile offenders avoid recidivism, because the dream does not offer concrete strategies of action that were useful in their situations. The dream does not take into account one's situation or the structural barriers that one might face. Elizabeth Strom and Greenbaum (2013) similarly found that homeowners who were foreclosed upon during the 2008 housing crisis continued to hold strong beliefs in the American Dream. They tended to blame themselves for the fact that the dream had not worked out for them personally. Working-class African American homebuyers were similarly drawn to the alluring ideology of the American Dream, and this ideology also fell short of providing the tools needed to overcome the structural barriers that they face.

Contrastingly, the culture of poverty theory, which has fallen out of favor with sociologists but remains a persistent notion in popular discourse, implies that poor Black people and other groups remain poor due to their adherence to alternative ideologies that conflict with the American Dream ideology. This idea that African Americans have an alternative, oppositional culture is exemplified by the "The Negro Family" report (Moynihan 1965) and was tied to the broader notion of a culture of poverty (Coward, Feagin and Williams 1974; Harvey and Reed 1996; Small, Harding and Lamont 2010). What I find instead, however, is that working-class African Americans are extremely dedicated to mainstream American ideals, just as Soyer (2016) found among poor Black juvenile offenders, and Strom and Greenbaum (2013) identified among foreclosed-upon homeowners. I posit that it is this very adherence to these mainstream values that leaves working-class African Americans open to further exploitation.

Lawrence Samuel (2012) argues that in recent decades, the American Dream has expanded to be inclusive of a more racially diverse population including African Americans, ultimately culminating in Barack Obama's heavy use of the dream narrative in his presidential campaigns. Instead, I argue that African Americans have long been some of the most devout adherents to the American Dream ideology, at least to a particular variant of the ideology, one that may incorporate a greater breadth of its historical tenets. Martin Luther King, Jr.'s "I Have a Dream" speech is a very famous historical example of an African American figure using the dream narrative rhetorically. One can go further back to 1936, turning to Langston Hughes' (2020) "Let America be America Again" for a poem that perfectly illustrates the paradox of belief in a dream that has always been exclusionary:

> Let America be the dream the dreamers dreamed—
> Let it be that great strong land of love
> Where never kings connive nor tyrants scheme
> That any man be crushed by one above.
> (It never was America to me.)

Here Hughes paints a picture of America as the land of the dream, in particular a dream of radical equality. Then, this secondary voice that interjects throughout the poem claims that America has never lived up to this dream. Later we learn that this marginalized voice—who speaks for the immigrant, the slave, the worker, and the indigenous person—is the one who "dreamt our basic dream." In 1936, Hughes understood Black people and other marginalized groups in the United States to be the keepers of the American Dream in its most noble form. Throughout my interviews, I found that African American working-class homebuyers today continue this legacy of devoting themselves to the dream, seemingly only more ardently as the obstacles to obtaining it become clearer to them.

At the same time, since the dream rests on ideals of equality, the visible presence of a minority population that has been all but barred from participation in the dream exposes it as a lie. James Baldwin (1965) argued that when the impossibility of the dream is made visible, it disturbs the ideological foundation of our society:

> Until the moment comes when we, the Americans, are able to accept the fact that my ancestors are both black and white, that on that continent we are trying to forge a new identity, that we need each other, that I am not a ward of America, I am not an object of missionary charity, I am one of the people who built the country—until this moment comes there is scarcely any hope for the American dream. If the people are denied participation in it, by their very presence they will wreck it.

When exposed in such compelling and vivid ways, the deep inequalities of American society are deadly for this ideology that justifies the American way of life.

Why Buy a Home?

African Americans have long suffered higher risks and lower financial returns from homeownership. The foreclosure crisis was simply the most recent twist in a long history of African American disadvantage in housing markets. Given this long history of disadvantage that makes homeownership such a risky prospect for African Americans, why would homeownership remain such an attractive form of investment for this group? Financial benefits do motivate some middle-income African Americans to pursue homeownership, but I argue that other incentives play a significant role in motivating this group. Homeownership is tied to the ideology of the American Dream. For African Americans in particular, success under the terms of the American Dream indicates full inclusion in mainstream American life and equal standing as American citizens. While African Americans face diminished financial returns in homeownership compared to Whites, the social benefits may be more compelling.

In *Facing Up to the American Dream,* Jennifer Hochschild (1996) argues that in the "psychologic of the American Dream," success demonstrates virtue. By extension, failure under the terms of the American Dream indicates some sort of personal flaw, either of moral fortitude or talents. The ideology of the American

Dream is fueled by a notion that any individual can reach their goals through diligent hard work. This industriousness is viewed as virtuous. The belief that the trappings of the American Dream are earned through hard work legitimizes the system. In contrast, failure indicates a lack of industriousness and is therefore seen as sinful. Since homeownership represents a concrete expression of the American Dream, failure and success in this arena carries with it a valence of virtue. To the extent that homeownership implies a sort of virtue, to experience foreclosure is to fall from grace. Foreclosure combines the stigma of bankruptcy—an inability to meet one's obligations—with the loss of a home. Despite historical exclusion from many facets of the American Dream, African Americans tend to endorse the beliefs associated with the ideology as strongly as Whites, and in some cases, more so (Hochschild 1996).

The homeownership version of the American Dream is one arena where African Americans, especially middle-class African Americans, have recently been able to participate in much greater numbers. From 1960 to 1980, the gap in homeownership rates between Whites and Blacks fell by 7.8 points (Collins and Margo 2001). Still, the racial gap in homeownership rates remains large. The homeownership rate for non-Hispanic Whites in the first quarter of 2016 was 72.1%, but only 45.1% for Blacks (Callis and Kresin 2012).

Through homeownership, many more African Americans have been able to participate in the American Dream recently, but not on equal terms. On average, African Americans pay one-third of a percentage point more on mortgage interest rates than Whites. In practice, this can lead to substantial disparities in wealth accumulation from homeownership. An African American homebuyer purchasing a median-priced home in 1999 would typically pay $11,756 more in interest over the course of a thirty-year loan. Furthermore, when the borrower makes a down payment of less than 20%, the lender usually requires private mortgage insurance; such insurance costs about $1,000 a year for a family buying a median-priced home. Households with less savings to draw upon for down payments—which disproportionately characterizes African American households—are more likely to fall into this category. Additionally, due to racial bias in housing markets, African Americans earn less equity in their homes. The value of a typical home owned by a White family rises $28,605 more than that of a Black family (Shapiro 2004). In other words, homeownership costs African Americans more and earns them less.

The Social Significance of Homeownership

Marker of Adulthood

Homeownership is discussed as both a marker of adulthood, an achievement that proves someone has reached a certain status in life, and as an opportunity for personal growth through greater responsibility. Emma likened owning a home to becoming a mother:

> I had Caleb late, kind of late. I was 27 when I had Caleb, and I had always been kind of a selfish, irresponsible person, because I knew I could be. I knew it wasn't going to affect anybody else. I didn't really see myself as an adult for that reason [...] and I was fine with that until I had Caleb, and then I felt pushed to be a better person, and I was happy to be pushed to be a better person, and so buying this house changes my perception of myself. Like I see myself as like an adult with responsibilities. I own a house, and I have a mortgage.

Emma's description of how motherhood changed her personality resonates with ideas about motherhood that Kathryn Edin and Maria Kefalas (2011) found among low-income single mothers in Philadelphia. These women felt that raising a child was an opportunity to gain social status and demonstrate their talents through meaningful work. Motherhood is also a status that comes with particular responsibilities. Similarly, homeownership can be a tool for becoming a responsible adult who embodies respectable middle-class values.

Other homebuyers who had not taken on other markers of adulthood (such as parenthood) saw homeownership as a first step towards becoming a responsible adult. In particular, homeownership is seen as a way to induce responsible financial habits. One single, childless homebuyer, Liam, said of homeownership: "It'll make me more financially conscious as far as my spending habits. Like right now I'm trying to learn how to budget myself, like how much I spend. I try not to go out as much." Saving for a down payment sometimes requires an aspiring homebuyer to make lifestyle changes, and Liam wants to make those changes. He looks forward to being more responsible, and he believes that owning a home will help him become more mature in this way. He anticipates that the activities required for homeownership will help him learn to be a better adult. Taking out a mortgage loan also forces a person to put a certain amount of money each month towards an investment, so it can induce behaviors that may be more financially beneficial than one's natural tendencies. Through the requirement to make monthly payments and save for a down payment, a mortgage loan can actually be a tool that provides a structure for personal growth and transformation into adulthood.

Interview participants viewed homeownership as a milestone tied to adulthood, as evidenced by the tendency for people to seek homeownership status by a certain age, even though there was no consensus on precisely when. The aspiring homebuyers varied a great deal in terms of age and the other markers of adulthood they had already attained (including children and marriage). Still, individual homebuyers sometimes expressed frustration around the notion that they had not attained homeownership by a particular age. For instance, Aisha recounted:

> Looking at my mom, looking at my brothers. My mom purchased her home, she was in her twenties, so it was like wow, I'm like behind. Not necessarily, but you know what I mean, and then my brother was like thirty, thirty-one,

> so if you figure it's like okay, I need to get this ball rolling, not because I have to, more so I want to, as an accomplishment.

Aisha was anxious to become a homeowner, not for the financial benefits, but because she perceives social pressure to attain this accomplishment by a certain age. Also, other homebuyers who had owned previously felt that losing that homeowner status was a setback in terms of their personal development and attaining life goals appropriate to their age, and not simply a financial concern. The social status associated with homeownership makes the effects of the foreclosure crisis particularly painful both for those who have lost their homes and for individuals who feel that they are coming of age without access to this significant marker of adult status.

Aspiring homebuyers like Aisha have a strong drive towards homeownership based on social rather than financial goals. This desire to achieve the social status that accompanies homeownership can lead aspiring homeowners to overlook some practical factors in the decision-making process. For instance, Aisha is a single mother with five children who currently lives with her mother. Her mother was helping out considerably with housework and childcare until her recent knee surgery, and even now she is able to watch the kids when Aisha runs errands. Aisha admits that having the kids on her own will be more difficult. Additionally, while she plans to wait until her mother recovers from the surgery before buying her own place and moving out, it is likely that her mother will continue to need some assistance as she ages. If Aisha moves, she will give up this mutually beneficial arrangement with her mother—as she cares for five children on her own and maintains a new home, Aisha will most likely still need to assist her mother with maintaining her own home. Yet Aisha remains steadfast in her conviction to take on a clearly less advantageous situation because she believes that homeownership is a status marker of a responsible and accomplished adult.

These aspiring homebuyers generally associated homeownership with successful and responsible adulthood. This association was made clear by the way they unfavorably compared renters to homeowners. For example, Jill remarked:

> I'm always concerned about rentals because people are transient. They're not setting roots. They're not invested in the community. Sometimes they don't bring progress. The homeowners of course are setting roots. They want to stay put. They are raising families. They are invested in the property; they are looking for good schools. They're making sure that there's adequate resources in the area.

The ways that Jill compares homeowners to renters all relate to a particular image of middle-class adult respectability. She implies that homeowners are more likely to have families and to be more concerned about the quality of schools. Jill regards homeowners as settled and therefore invested, full citizens in their communities.

She wants to become a homeowner to prove to herself and others that she can take on these qualities. She also wants to surround herself with a community of other invested citizen homeowners who will work together to improve their neighborhood and create a better living environment for their children.

This belief that communities with more homeowners are better places to live was widespread among the homebuyers. There are, of course, many practical reasons why one might prefer such a neighborhood, but their understanding of why homeowners make better neighbors underscored this notion that homeowners are more respectable moral citizens. Additionally, the homebuyers want to be a part of this kind of moral community.

The aspiring homeowners could envision the process of homebuying as enculturation into such a community, meaning that they see the homebuying process as a process of socialization into an ideal middle-class lifestyle. One homebuyer mentioned that he was particularly pleased to have bought his home through Habitat for Humanity because he felt that the structure of the program helped prepare him for homeownership. Andrew, a 29-year-old mail clerk, explained:

> We went through a seminar and then we had to go through a credit check. [...] When we were finally accepted into the program, we knew we wanted to take it on as fast as possible, so we started running through our hours. We had to have a total of 500 hours to actually get the home, but we had to get 165 hours just to be able to choose which home we wanted to select. So we went through the 165 hours very fast and after we chose which home [and] we had to finish our hours. [...] And I really enjoyed the construction hours, because the construction hours actually taught you how to maintain [a home], so that really, really was awesome for me. And you get to meet some of the people that are already working there, who have been doing it for a long time, construction guys, so I enjoyed it. I can pick their brains. Another thing I liked about the Habitat process was when it snowed really heavy out, our job was not just working on our home but also helping others. So we would shovel out our driveway but we'd also shovel out each neighbor on each side's driveway, and the walkways and the sidewalk. It really showed the community that we cared, which in turn kind of transferred over to me, so that's what I do now, with my neighbors. I shovel their driveway as well as mine, and I also shovel the sidewalk. It was a learning experience for me and helps me to be a better neighbor.

He felt that the Habitat for Humanity program taught him vital lessons about home maintenance and how to be a better neighbor. His experience, and his own framing of it, exemplifies one aspect of what underlies the public policy focus on homeownership, which Keeanga-Yamahtta Taylor (2019) argues is the goal of fostering particular values among citizens. Andrew believes that successful homeownership requires a do-it-yourself type of responsibility coupled with a community-oriented attitude. He values this program for teaching him the necessary skills to be an independent homeowner, responsible for his own private property, and able to take care of it in a hands-on manner. At the same time, he values the community service element. To be a really great homeowner requires being able to help others in your community in addition to being responsible for the upkeep of your own home. In this way, the ability to be a good neighbor represents another level of adult responsibility and respectable middle-class values. Furthermore, it shows how connected the notion is to the seeming paradox of American ideology that values independence and contributions to social good (Bellah et al. 2007).

Control

The American Dream of homeownership derives from an ideal of personal freedom associated with the ownership of land. It is logical, therefore, that homebuyers seek homeownership in order to exert greater control over their living space. Whether they rent or live in a family home, adults who do not own their own home are subjected to the actions and preferences of others in their own living space. Home, in the American view, is a refuge from the world, "a haven in a heartless world" (Lasch 1995). Adults who must abide by expectations, rules, standards, and goals set by others outside the home look forward to retiring to their own space where they can be in control. By contrast, this "ownness" associated with homeownership is incomplete in a house or apartment that one does not own. For instance, Anthony raised two ways in which he felt a lack of control as a renter:

> Basically, just the privacy is one. Knowing that it's ours, that we don't have to answer to a landlord, because a couple times the landlord, sometimes they'll come and fix things, sometimes they don't. So, the comfort of knowing that its mine is the number one thing. And to feel safe, that's another one.

The fact that landlords are supposed to maintain properties creates two areas of concern for Anthony. On one hand, Anthony feels that the landlord does not always maintain the property properly. As a homeowner, though, Anthony would have full control and responsibility for home repairs. He seeks homeownership in part for this opportunity for self-determination.

On the other hand, when the landlord does make repairs, this requires access to Anthony's home and it compromises the privacy of the home. Anthony elaborated that this particular landlord often comes unannounced:

> They just pop up, we could be at home on a Saturday morning, we'll hear something outside and go outside, it's him, and I'm like, you didn't call to tell nobody anything. We don't know what you're doing. Sometimes my kids be

> in the house by they self and they hear things, and it be him, and I have to go out there with them to see what's going on, and it's the landlord.

One complicating factor in this situation is that Anthony is not an official tenant at this apartment. Because his fiancée (and the mother of his children) uses a rental subsidy for this apartment, Anthony cannot be on the lease. Clearly, this situation must contribute to his anxiety about the landlord arriving at his home unannounced. Both the regular invasions of privacy and the regulations regarding residents make this apartment much less than a home for Anthony and his family. Living in a rental apartment can dramatically hamper one's ability to experience the freedom that is at the core of the ideology of the American Dream.

Furthermore, many aspiring homebuyers were currently living with other family members, sometimes their parents, when they would have preferred to have their own household. Liam said that when he has his own home, he looks forward to various freedoms:

> [to] move around as I please, because when you live with your parents you have to abide by a set of rules, like—if you go out, you have to be mindful when you go out or when you come back in, or where you're at or whatever the case may be, so I'm like—I can just—there I can just come and go as I please. If I don't want to do something one day, I don't have to do it, or whatever. I can decorate how I want, invite whoever I want over.

Liam is 25 years old and single, so one could imagine someone in his situation choosing to rent an apartment in order to gain this freedom from his parents. But for Liam, renting an apartment would not symbolize freedom in the same way as buying a house. Furthermore, spending money on rent could cause him to have to delay attaining homeownership even further, which he regards as an important signifier of successful adulthood. Many of the aspiring homebuyers were willing to endure significant sacrifices, even those that curtail their sense of freedom and control of their living space, in order to achieve their goal of homeownership eventually.

Finally, in the space of one's home one can exercise certain freedoms that are not afforded in other kinds of spaces. One aspiring homebuyer who currently rents, Emmanuel, explained that he wants to buy a home "because I buy into the idea of having the American Dream of having somewhere where you can do what you want when you want." Another aspiring homebuyer, Bridget, argued that buying a home rather than renting would provide her with greater freedom. She explained why she wanted to become a homeowner:

> I like the freedom of I can water my grass when I want to. I can put a swimming pool in my yard if I want to. I don't need permission from a

> landlord, or I don't live in a building with people and children running over my head, or my children are running over somebody else's head.

For Bridget, the significance of having greater control over her living space is not the ability to make specific changes or engage in any particular activity in her home. Instead, owning the home means that she will have complete freedom in that space. She believes that by owning a home she will not be beholden to anyone else, at least in the confines of her home. Homeownership is a prerequisite for experiencing this kind of freedom. In sum, the Jeffersonian ideal at the core of the American Dream is ultimately about having a space that you can control as a private citizen, and for many, that space is embodied in a home.

Racial Uplift

A few homebuyers saw their personal goal of homeownership as explicitly tied to a form of racial uplift similar to what ethnographers Monique Taylor (2002), Mary Pattillo (2007), and Michelle Boyd (2008) describe among Black gentrifiers who bought homes in predominately Black neighborhoods. Taylor, Pattillo, and Boyd each conducted ethnographic studies of relatively stable middle-class Black neighborhoods including Harlem, New York, and Bronzeville, Chicago. In these neighborhoods, middle-class (and upper-middle-class) homeowners saw their investment in their homes as an investment in the Black community. It is important to note that highly stable middle-class Black communities of this kind are fairly unusual. Many African American homebuyers do not have access to this kind of place. Furthermore, the example of Bronzeville demonstrates how after the foreclosure crisis some communities of this type no longer appear as stable. Since the early 2000s, the neighborhood suffered from high rates of subprime loans, foreclosures and, ultimately, a 20% decline in home values from 2007 to 2009 (Hyra and Rugh 2016). I found that many African American homebuyers who were not buying in predominately Black, middle-class communities associated successful attainment of homeownership with a more general sense that they could contribute to the standing of the group by participating more fully in the American Dream. Generally, the American Dream gives a moral value to material success; for African Americans, personal material success can also be connected to the dream of equality.

While many homebuyers were considering Black neighborhoods, these were almost never their first choice; yet some spoke about the benefits of investing in Black neighborhoods through homeownership. Martin was unusual among the homebuyers I interviewed because he said that if all other aspects were equal, he would actually prefer a predominately Black area to a majority White area:

> I would say if I would be able to find an area that's more so Black that is a nice area, I would think I would be leaning towards moving to that type of

> area because I'm a person where I'm very hard on well-to-do Blacks, the folks who earned a bunch of money, the celebrities, the athletes, and they don't really do anything for their own folk. So, if I would be able to find something in a majority Black area, I would love to do that, to help my own, to get a place to live and so forth. Whatever little bit I can do with what little money I make, so that's mine.

For Martin, homeownership represents an opportunity to make an investment that will help Black communities directly. Martin was unusual among the homebuyers in how positively he viewed buying a home in a predominately Black area. By contrast, many of the homebuyers stated a strong preference for buying in racially mixed areas.

Elijah also expressed an interest in racial uplift through homeownership in Black neighborhoods. Elijah grew up on the South Side of Chicago in the Chatham neighborhood. Interestingly, he moved to Oak Lawn twelve years ago when he got married, and he now wishes to move back to Chicago. He has two daughters, aged 13 and 10. He likes Oak Lawn, and he describes it as multicultural, clean, and quiet. Still, he told me that he is now considering a move back to the city to buy a home:

> I would love to live in the city. [...] It has to start somewhere, so I feel if you want to make changes you can either help or you can complain about it, and I would love to help the community. [...] I was raised in the city.

Elijah provides a strong example of a homebuyer who expects to be able to improve a Black neighborhood by investing through homeownership. He sees his choice to buy in a Black neighborhood as a way to give back to his own community, but other factors have pushed him towards this choice.

Additionally, I asked why he had decided against Oak Lawn since he had described it in such a positive light. Elijah explained:

> Well, I would love to live in Oak Lawn, but I want to be a homeowner that's able to live a comfortable life and not have every dollar that I make going toward my mortgage or my taxes. Unfortunately, living in Oak Lawn, the taxes are a little high.

It is typically more expensive to buy a home in a racially diverse suburb than in a predominately Black neighborhood in Chicago. While Elijah can afford to rent in a suburb with demographics and amenities that he appreciates, becoming a homeowner there would be a financial stretch.

For Elijah, the goal of homeownership overshadows all other concerns because he views it as the fulfillment of the American Dream:

> You can pass [a home] down to kids, it gives—like they say the American Dream, and just knowing that you've accomplished a goal of being a homeowner, I think that's more important than anything.

While Elijah frames the choice in terms of the ability to support the community where he was raised in a new way, he is also considering moving back to Chatham because this compromise will allow him to attain the status of homeowner and achieve success in terms of the American Dream. Through these stated interests in contributing to racial progress by investing in homes in Black neighborhoods, Elijah and Martin exemplified how some homebuyers understood their home purchase in terms of racial uplift.

Many of the other homebuyers explicitly stated a desire to move to racially mixed areas. In particular, homebuyers were interested in racially mixed, middle-class suburbs. A high value was placed on living near other homeowners who they believed would share middle-class values. For instance, when I asked Nancy what kind of neighborhood she wanted to live in, she replied, "I want a combination platter." She explained:

> A combination platter meaning race. I have to be straight up and honest with you. [...] You want your yard looking nice? So do I. Oops. It doesn't matter the color. Don't be offended if I don't want to be next to you because you got garbage throwed all over.

Nancy believes that in a racially diverse area she will be more likely to share values and cultural norms with her neighbors than in an all-Black neighborhood. The most significant norms to her are ideas about how to maintain the outside appearance of the home. Nancy wants to live near other homeowners who share the same norms about home maintenance and use of outdoor space around the home.

I asked Nancy "Why does the combination platter work?"

She replied:

> For the simple reason, these people—regardless of your race—we all would have something in common versus all Blacks [and]—Oh, let me say this—this ghetto mentality, some of us [have]. And when I look at a racially diverse area, we have something in community because we all want to try to do the best we can to live together as one, regardless of their race. But I found with a lot of my own people, some of them [are] just not on the same level. And when you want to do the best you can, then we're trying to be White. It's the truth, and that's the way they look at it. [...] So, when you're in a diverse area, all of us probably was raised differently, but we got that one common goal... that we're living in this area and we want the best for our families, versus all of our Black—well, we don't do this, and we don't do that, no.

> Speak for yourself. That ain't me. I didn't raise mine that way, so it means a lot to be in a diverse area.

Nancy associates neighborhood racial diversity with class and cultural homogeneity. She wishes to live with people who she believes are more like her in terms of their worldview, behaviors, and interests. She is the kind of person who wants to maintain an impeccable lawn and follow other middle-class suburban values. Therefore, she finds it deeply frustrating to be geographically surrounded by people with different cultural norms. Her frustration is exacerbated by a sense that she is racially stereotyped as sharing norms with people who do not hold the same class aspirations and values. Nancy also associates racially diverse communities with striving for success and achieving upward mobility. Her belief in bettering oneself through personal initiative can be seen as a part of the American Dream. For homebuyers like Nancy, buying a home in a middle-class, racially diverse area is part of the American Dream, and rather than seeing this as a betrayal of the Black community, she feels betrayed by those who associate improvement with non-Blackness.

Therefore, some homebuyers took a broader view on the connection between homeownership and racial uplift. For instance, one married couple, Sandra and Jaheem, spoke about how they appreciated that the homebuyer education class they took in Roseland addressed credit-building techniques, because they felt that this knowledge was not widespread enough in the African American community:

> *Jaheem*: The classes were very informative.
>
> *Sandra*: They were helpful too. And we go back in the books that we got from the classes and look for stuff. So, yeah. It made us pay attention to our credit reports.
>
> *Jaheem*: I mean, it's sad to say that this is not commonplace in the Black community. It hasn't been going on for years and years. In small groups it has. But on the mass scale it has not.
>
> [...]
>
> *Interviewer:* Is there any [other] sort of assistance [from NHS] that you could imagine would have been really helpful?
>
> *Sandra*: Credit building. I think I wrote that down in the margins when they were asking in class what classes would you want more of, and like I said, I think for us within the community, credit-building classes. A lot of African Americans don't know how important it is to keep your credit in check. I think if there were classes about that specifically, I'm thinking more people would attend them because it's so important. Especially if you're trying to get a car or a home purchase, I know it's really important.

They are pleased that this class gave them more information about credit building and would like to see more classes offered specifically on this skill because it will eventually help them purchase a home, which is their own personal life goal. Additionally, they have a deep sense of community and it remains important to them that other African Americans are able to achieve the goals associated with homeownership. The Roseland Homebuyers Education seminar that they attended is in a predominately Black community and the attendees were nearly all Black. They appreciated the class not simply for their own sake but also because they saw other African Americans learning about credit building, which is a necessary behavior for achieving the American Dream of homeownership. Sandra and Jaheem see credit building as a tool to improve the situation of their family and for the betterment of their community. Successfully building credit demonstrates the virtues associated with the American Dream in its own right. Therefore, these credit-building efforts can take on a missionary fervor both on the part of those who spread the gospel of financial literacy and among new converts.

For African American aspiring homebuyers, success at the American Dream of homeownership is directly tied to the American Dream of equality. Bridget explained that she wanted to buy a home that her children could one day inherit. This moral obligation that she felt as a parent carries extra weight because she feels that attaining this goal is more unusual in the Black community:

> I need to leave my child something. I'm a spiritual person, and the Bible says that we are to leave our offspring an inheritance. And I started thinking, how many cultures really do that? And I can't say from the colored side of me it's not often that we do that. And I'm like, well, I don't want to be like that. I want my children to live somewhere where nobody can tell them to get out of their home. It's their home. It's going to require upkeep, taxes paid, different things like that. It's not to spoil them from knowing that they need to get out in the real world and fend for themselves, but it is to make their lives a little easier because I don't have anybody passing me down or handing me anything, so that's where that decision [came from] of, you know what? I need to get something to leave my children.

Bridget sees her own personal success in the arena of homeownership as contributing to progress for the Black community more broadly. In her family and the community that surrounds her, homeownership is not widespread, but Bridget feels that it should be. Homeownership is important to her because she believes it will give her children greater freedom and opportunity than she had. In this case, success at the American Dream of homeownership carries moral weight both personally and for the wider community. The ideology of the American Dream makes individual success a moral good, and Bridget connects this to her spirituality. Aspiring homebuyers like Bridget believe deeply in the moral value of individual economic success. Furthermore, personal success for African American aspiring homebuyers can be seen as improving the standing of the broader Black community. In this way, the purchase of a home can be interpreted as progress towards two versions of the American Dream: the personal American Dream of homeownership and the community-oriented American Dream of equality.

Conclusion

The ideology of the American Dream gives homeownership its special significance as a highly visible sign of success in an endeavor that has moral importance. This link between homeownership and the American Dream meant that those who were foreclosed upon in the crisis experienced financial, social, and emotional cost. In particular, African Americans were disproportionately affected by the foreclosure crisis. During this period, African Americans, who have historically been excluded from the American Dream of homeownership, were allowed greater access to the American Dream, only to have this dream shattered by predatory mortgage lending practices.

As a result, African American aspiring homebuyers are currently highly aware of the potential pitfalls of homeownership in the wake of the foreclosure crisis. The respondents in this study represent the group committed to the dream of homeownership despite many challenges. This population is important to study because many are at a crucial threshold in the process of solidifying their middle-class status. Many of these homebuyers are on the precarious edge of the middle class, and they hope that homeownership will be a tool for securing their economic future. Since their adherence to the goal of homeownership is so strong, studying this group provides an opportunity to examine why homeownership remains a powerful ideal even when it is a risky investment. For middle-income African American homebuyers, homeownership is both a means and an end to personal fulfillment within the terms of this dream.

In contrast to the notion that the American Dream was only recently of relevance to African Americans or that most African Americans hold oppositional ideologies to the dream, I find that many working-class African American homebuyers adhere to the ideology of the dream strongly. Furthermore, this strong adherence to the American Dream makes them more vulnerable to financial distress caused by a racially biased housing market.

The homebuyers in this study believe that the process of buying a home will help them develop responsible characteristics that will carry over into other aspects of life. Homeownership signifies adult status and accomplishment, but it is also seen as step that will shape the individual and prepare them for greater accomplishments and responsibility. Researchers have found that homeowners invest more in social capital (DiPasquale and Glaeser 1999) and are more likely to join community improvement groups (Rossi and Weber 1996).

Furthermore, owning a home symbolizes success in a morally important endeavor: homeowners are viewed as virtuous citizens. Finally, a home provides a space to realize the American Dream because it is the site where freedom can actually be enjoyed. For all of these social and moral reasons, homeownership maintains its place as an important goal for many middle-income African Americans. These moral and social benefits of homeownership take precedence over other factors when deciding whether to pursue this goal. They also make the loss of homeowner status through foreclosure more painful. For African Americans, the ability to attain and keep a home is tied to success at the American Dream of homeownership and the dream of equality.

The aspiring homeowners in this study proactively brought up the notion of the American Dream with remarkable frequency, both by using this term and by alluding to the tenets of the ideology. It was clearly central to their own understanding of why they were pursuing homeownership. Although homeownership can be a relatively risky and less rewarding investment for this population, these homebuyers remained committed to buying a home as the dream of homeownership can also be interpreted as contributing to racial progress and the dream of equality. Therefore, the racially disproportionate effects of the foreclosure crisis undercut both the American Dream of homeownership and the dream of equality. Homebuyers' ideological commitment to this dream that emphasizes agency also obscures very real structural barriers to attaining it. In the next chapter, I discuss the structural barriers African Americans face in achieving homeownership in more detail, as well as the social consequences of these delayed dreams.

References

Baldwin, James. 1965. "The American Dream and the American Negro." The New York Times, March 7, 1965: 32–33.

Bellah, Robert N., Richard Madsen, William M. Sullivan, Ann Swidler, and Steven M. Tipton. 2007. *Habits of the Heart: Individualism and Commitment in American Life*. Berkeley: University of California Press.

Boyd, Michelle R. 2008. *Jim Crow Nostalgia: Reconstructing Race in Bronzeville*. Minneapolis: University of Minnesota Press.

Callis, Robert R., and Melissa Kresin. 2012. "Residential Vacancies and Homeownership in the First Quarter 2012." US Census Bureau News: CB12-60. April 30, 2012. www.census.gov/housing/hvs/files/qtr112/q112press.pdf.

Collins, William J., and Robert A. Margo. 2001. "Race and Home Ownership: A Century-Long View." *Explorations in Economic History* 38(1): 68–92.

Coward, Barbara E., Joe R. Feagin, and J. Allen Williams. 1974. "The Culture of Poverty Debate: Some Additional Data." *Social Problems* 21(5): 621–634. https://doi.org/10.2307/799638.

Cullen, Jim. 2004. *The American Dream: A Short History of an Idea that Shaped a Nation*. New York: Oxford University Press.

DiPasquale, Denise, and Edward L. Glaeser. 1999. "Incentives and Social Capital: Are Homeowners Better Citizens?" *Journal of Urban Economics* 45(2): 354–384. https://doi.org/10.1006/juec.1998.2098.

Edin, Kathryn, and Maria Kefalas. 2011. *Promises I Can Keep: Why Poor Women Put Motherhood Before Marriage*. Berkeley: University of California Press.

Harvey, David L., and Michael H. Reed. 1996. "The Culture of Poverty: An Ideological Analysis." *Sociological Perspectives* 39(4): 465–495. https://doi.org/10.2307/1389418.

Hochschild, Jennifer L. 1996. *Facing Up to the American Dream: Race, Class, and the Soul of the Nation*. Princeton: Princeton University Press.

Hughes, Langston. 2020. *The Collected Poems of Langston Hughes*. New York: Vintage.

Hyra, Derek, and Jacob S. Rugh. 2016. "The U.S. Great Recession: Exploring Its Association with Black Neighborhood Rise, Decline and Recovery." *Urban Geography* 37(5): 700–726. https://doi.org/10.1080/02723638.2015.1103994.

Johnson, Heather Beth. 2015. *The American Dream and the Power of Wealth: Choosing Schools and Inheriting Inequality in the Land of Opportunity*, 2nd ed. New York: Routledge.

Lasch, Christopher. 1995. *Haven in a Heartless World: The Family Besieged*. New York: W. W. Norton & Company.

Moynihan, Daniel Patrick. 1965. "The Negro Family: The Case for National Action." Washington, D.C.: US Government Publishing Office.

Pattillo, Mary. 2007. *Black on the Block: The Politics of Race and Class in the City*. Chicago: University of Chicago Press.

Rossi, Peter H, and Eleanor Weber. 1996. "The Social Benefits of Homeownership: Empirical Evidence from National Surveys." *Housing Policy Debate* 7(1): 1–35. https://doi.org/10.1080/10511482.1996.9521212.

Samuel, Lawrence R. 2012. *The American Dream: A Cultural History*. Syracuse: Syracuse University Press.

Shapiro, Thomas M. 2004. *The Hidden Cost of Being African American: How Wealth Perpetuates Inequality*. New York: Oxford University Press.

Small, Mario Luis, David J. Harding, and Michèle Lamont. 2010. "Introduction: Reconsidering Culture and Poverty." *The Annals of the American Academy of Political and Social Science* 629(1): 6–27.

Soyer, Michaela. 2016. *A Dream Denied: Incarceration, Recidivism, and Young Minority Men in America*. Berkeley: University of California Press.

Strom, Elizabeth, and Susan Greenbaum. 2013. "Still the 'American Dream'? Views of Home Ownership in the Wake of the Foreclosure Crisis." In *Home: International Perspectives on Culture, Identity, and Belonging*, edited by M. Kusenbach and K. E. Paulsen. Frankfurt: Peter Lang GmbH, Internationaler Verlag der Wissenschaften.

Taylor, Keeanga-Yamahtta. 2019. *Race for Profit: How Banks and the Real Estate Industry Undermined Black Homeownership*. Chapel Hill: University of North Carolina Press.

Taylor, Monique M. 2002. *Harlem: Between Heaven and Hell*. Minneapolis: University of Minnesota Press.

Willie, Charles V., and Richard J. Reddick. 2010. *A New Look at Black Families*, 6th ed. Lanham, MD: Rowman & Littlefield.

3

HOMEOWNERSHIP DELAYED

Hannah works as a teacher's assistant. Eleven years ago, she moved into a two-bedroom, one-bathroom apartment with her husband and her two-year-old daughter. They now have three girls, aged twelve, nine, and seven, and Hannah feels that "there's absolutely no room." Furthermore, she explained, "It's driving us crazy to have a preteen" with just one bathroom. To put it mildly, Hannah wants to move because her current residence no longer meets the needs of her growing family of five.

Households change as children are born and then again as they leave to form their own households. These changes often fuel people's desires to move. Financial constraints caused families to delay their homebuying process, often for several years after they first felt the desire to relocate. Hannah and her husband began searching for a home after they had their second child. She felt that the children "didn't have a real place to play" because they lacked a backyard and they "didn't really feel safe in the neighborhood to go walking and riding bikes." Then, during the economic downturn in 2008, they encountered financial trouble, which delayed their homebuying process. By the time of our interview in 2015, their situation had improved because Hannah was able to find full-time work. Hannah and her husband finally bought a home almost exactly a year later, in February 2016, eight years after she had first decided that her family needed more space. In the intervening time, their two children aged eight years and another was born. This family's space constraints continued and their children had other needs, including schooling. Moreover, as their daughters became teenagers who could leave the home unsupervised, safety concerns increased.

In general, African Americans often buy homes later than Whites owing to the many extra obstacles they face. For many of the homebuyers in this study, frustrations resulted from not being able to purchase a home at the time that it was most needed for their family. Families with young children need more space as they have more children and their children grow. Other needs change as families grow, including need for schools. Delayed homebuying meant that some families had to find alternative strategies to decouple home choice from school choice. Additionally, homeownership is often sought as a milestone of meeting a certain life stage. Meeting this milestone is important to African Americans, but it was unattainable for many of the homebuyers in this study. Consequently, the homebuyers experienced a sense of inadequacy and anxiety around failing to meet this milestone by a particular age or life stage.

African Americans are more likely to live in multigenerational households, and the homebuying decision was often a moment when family structures were reconsidered and renegotiated. Multigenerational living arrangements are used, in part, as a strategy to prepare financially for homeownership. Because multigenerational households were common among this group, households were making decisions not just about where to move but also about who would be moving into the new home. Research on housing tends to take the household as a given unit, but in reality, households have a process of formation that can be concurrent with the housing search process.

Many middle-income African American homebuyers have to delay homebuying for a significant amount of time after changes in their family structure make a move highly desirable. Homebuyers usually stated that they developed a desire to buy a home when they reached adulthood, married, divorced, had children, or when their children reached a particular age, but they often were not able to make a purchase at that time. Some households in this study had wanted to relocate to a new home for several years. Some homebuyers moved in with another family at this point in order to save money for the home purchase. During this waiting period, their families continued to age and their needs would change, complicating the process of preparing for homeownership. Ultimately, delayed homebuying complicates the homebuying process and limits the benefits that African American families receive from homeownership.

The homebuying decision was often a moment when family structures were reconsidered and renegotiated. In other words, some homebuyers were still deciding which family members would be relocating into the home that they sought to buy as they began the homebuying process. Multigenerational living arrangements are used, in part, as a strategy to prepare financially for homeownership. Because multigenerational households were common among this group, households were making decisions not just about where to move but also about who would be moving into the new home. For these reasons, deciding on household composition is often part of the homebuying process for this group. Additionally, delayed homebuying meant that families had to find alternative strategies for attaining access to quality schools. Because of these delays, school choice was often already decoupled from home choice by the time households were able to buy a home.

Credit problems were the most common hurdle to homeownership that delayed purchasing.

Traditional Life Cycle and Residential Mobility

Previous research suggests that as households go through a typical life cycle, they tend to move at certain predictable points in time in order to find dwelling spaces that meet their new needs. Peter Rossi developed a model to explain residential mobility based on his extensive interviews with residents in the Philadelphia area in the 1950s. According to Rossi (1980), each household has a set of needs and a level of satisfaction with how their current home is meeting those needs. These needs and complaints can be about the dwelling structure, the environment surrounding the home, or the location of the home. Housing needs change as a household goes through a typical life cycle, and the most important need that changes through this life cycle is space (for example, as a household grows, more space is required). For the Philadelphians whom Rossi studied, most moves happened in the decade following the initial formation of the household. At the time that Rossi conducted his study, this typically meant that two young people married and left their parents' homes to form a new family. Following this traditional view of household formation and changes over the life course, one can imagine a few different stages in which the needs of households would change from initial family formation to aging.

Traditional Life Course Stages and Housing Needs

In some respects, the needs of families and life cycle changes have remained fairly consistent since Rossi wrote in the 1950s. For many of the homebuyers in this study, frustrations resulted from not being able to purchase a home at the time it was most needed for their family. Many homebuyers wanted to get more space for their growing families by moving out of a rental apartment or a home that they shared with other relatives into their own single-family home. In this

TABLE 3.1 Life Course Stages and Housing Needs

Life Course Stage	*Housing Needs*
Young single person or childless couple	Small space, affordability
Family with young children	More space, access to parks and recreation facilities
Family with school-age children	More space, quality schools
Aging adults	Less space, fewer stairs, access to services for seniors

respect, Hannah's experience is similar to the families studied by Rossi (1980). Households change as children are born and then again as they leave to form their own households. Of course, not all families are able to act on their desires to move as they grow and age. Rossi pointed out that the most frustrated families are often those with young children who do not have the financial resources to obtain more spacious housing when they need it. At the same time, older households without children often find it difficult to leave homes that are larger than they need. Overall, this creates a mismatch between family size and home size. Many homebuyers in this study felt these life-cycle-related constraints on the ability to move into housing that matched household needs.

Delay in Homebuying

African Americans typically become homeowners later than Whites. Researchers at the Urban Institute found that for people who turned 60 or 61 years old between 2003 and 2015, 85% of White homeowners bought their first home before 35, comparted to 53% of Black homeowners (Hyun Choi, McCargo, and Goodman 2019). Nancy Denton (2001) used the 1960, 1970, 1980, and 1990 Integrated Public Use Microdata Series to compare homeownership rates over time for heads of households aged 25 to 74 years old. At every age between 40 and 60, the Black probability of homeownership is similar to what was achieved by Whites a decade earlier. For example, at age 50, Blacks have a probability of 0.74 of owning a home, while Whites achieve a similar probability of homeownership by age 40. A decade can make a large difference in terms of the stage in the life course when families are buying homes. In particular, for families with children this delay in homebuying affects their ability to obtain resources at key points in children's development.

In many ways, African American aspiring homebuyers find themselves in a similar situation to what Jane Zavisca (2013) describes among young adults in post-Soviet Russia. Following the end of state socialism in Russia, residents of state-owned apartments gained property rights, leading to near-universal owner-occupied housing. But, a couple of decades later, a younger generation of Russians found themselves unable to buy or rent their own homes. By 2009, over half of Russians in their twenties and thirties lived with extended family. These adults, crowded into small apartments with their parents and other extended family, felt stifled by the lack of autonomy and did not feel that they had appropriate space to raise children. These young Russians seemed to frame the problem mostly as a practical matter, one that harmed their wellbeing and their ability to provide a comfortable life for their children. For the aspiring homebuyers in this study, delayed homeownership was a practical problem for the same reasons, but they also experienced this as a personal failing, due to the strong cultural expectation in the United States that homeownership is a milestone that middle-class adults must achieve.

Many of the homebuyers felt frustrated with how long they had waited to buy a home. For example, Ruth began seriously considering homeownership at a late age. She had already raised her only child while living in her parents' home. Her son is an adult now with his own family. She perceived a deep sense of lagging behind previous generations in terms of what they were able to achieve by her age:

> It's just a sign of the times as far as the economy. It's not being turned around as quickly and when I say not being turned around, I mean, high school, college or trade, come out, get a decent working wage job, then go on to the next phase. Nowadays the next phase, you might not get to the next phase for another twenty years. Because I'm a good example of that because of how I'm forty-seven and I just started really thinking about buying a home, really [only] within the past seven or eight years, because I was able—I made that turnaround. I had gone to school, worked, and finally landed a pretty decent job. I think I can be able to do this.

Ruth uses the term "turnaround" two different ways. In her first usage, it means being able to get to the next stage in life. A lot of these stages simply take more time now than they did a generation ago.

As Ruth acknowledges, building a stable household required more schooling for her than it had for her parents' generation. At the same time, procuring those advanced degrees now required a larger financial investment. Gathering the resources to make it through the steps that Ruth associates with successful adulthood took a long time. By the time Ruth was able to seriously pursue homeownership, she had already raised her son and was therefore in a different position from a more traditional first-time homebuyer. She also uses the term "turnaround" in the sense of making a complete change and setting her life course on a different trajectory. She felt that she had made a "turnaround" in her life, so that she could finally achieve this socially important goal of homeownership.

Children are one of the main factors that cause household needs to change over the life course. Some families who had been considering relocation for a long time mentioned that their needs regarding schools changed during the time that they had prepared for homeownership. For instance, one married couple whom I interviewed together, Sandra and Jaheem, explained that eighteen years earlier they had been considering a move to the north suburbs in order to place their kids in better schools:

> *Jaheem*: When the kids were really young, I was talking to her about schools—northern suburbs, I'm talking. It's a high school. It's really highly ranked. I can't remember the name. I was talking about maybe renting an apartment that far north. I'm not sure if it's like Zion or anything like that, but it's far north. And not having the expense of paying $300,000, $400,000 for a house, not being able to afford that, but being able to afford an apartment in

that school district—yeah, we decided against it. During that time, Internet searching really wasn't what it was.

Sandra: Right [laughs].

Jaheem: Twenty years ago, almost, and so the type of information that was available now wasn't available then. So, I was just mainly going off the top of my head, knowing where it was. And so, we were discussing, [how we could] get an apartment up there, but the information I guess wasn't available then to search for it. We could have talked to a realtor [...] but to do the self-searching, it wasn't the same as it is now.

In the time that Jaheem and Sandra were thinking about relocating, their family changed. At the same time, broader circumstances changed. Jaheem and Sandra point to something about the search process that has greatly improved: access to information about available housing units. One common form of racial discrimination is simply not giving minorities information about available units. Landlords, sellers, and real estate agents have less ability to control what information people get now that listings are widely available online. Almost all the homebuyers did substantial searching online. Jaheem and Sandra thought that finding a place in a top school district in the northern suburbs would be easier with the current tools than it was years before, but now their needs had changed. On the day of this interview, their oldest daughter took the ACT college entrance exam. She was nearly done with school and possibly ready to move out of their home.

Instead of moving to the north suburbs, Sandra and Jaheem were now considering purchasing the house they had rented on the South Side since 2004. Sandra said of the house:

> It's like a grandma. It's old and she's breaking down a bit, leaky ceiling, but we're used to her. Well, not all of the time, still creaks in the night and I'm like—but the kids are acclimated here. We've had a child that's gone from 8 to 19, so we're known in the school circles, everybody knows us. We know all the teachers, and they know—they've learned to get from A to B to C to D to this person's house to back home before curfew, so it's like we're comfortable here, but I don't know if we want to stay here.

While the couple had wanted to raise their children in a different neighborhood context at one time, they had found ways to handle their circumstances in the city. Even if the situation was less than ideal, the whole family had grown accustomed to their neighborhood and their home.

Furthermore, their children were making their way through their schooling years and would be moving on in the near future. Jaheem explained that while at one time they may have felt crunched for space in this house, circumstances had changed. "For us at this age we don't need a four or five bedroom—we don't need that type of expense or size right now, and I just think we're used to it." As

Sandra and Jaheem buy a home for the first time, after years in an overcrowded home, they realize that they will actually be in a position to downsize in the near future. Sandra and Jaheem are an example of a family who would have prioritized school choice as a part of their home choice if they had been able to buy a home earlier. Delayed homebuying meant that their needs changed by the time they were prepared to make a purchase, and they were not able to use residential mobility as a means to access high-quality schools.

Credit Histories and Delayed Homebuying

This delay in homebuying may relate to the fact that African American households have substantially less wealth than White households (Shapiro 2006). The racial wealth gap contributes to the credit issues experienced by middle-income African American homebuyers, which in turn makes it difficult to qualify for a mortgage loan. It is one thing to choose to take on debt to fund investments, but households that have little or no wealth must use debt to handle crisis situations, and this creates negative wealth. In turn, credit problems can lead to substantial delays in homebuying. Aspiring homebuyers must pay off debt, build positive credit histories, and then wait years for their credit report to reflect the change in their financial behavior.

For example, Sandra and Jaheem said their credit problems resulted from being overwhelmed by other priorities in their lives and not fully appreciating the importance of good credit.

> *Sandra*: Yeah, not really focusing on it at an early age. It wasn't a lot of bad credit, it was just little things that were bad. [...] It was just little small annoying things that drag your credit score down, things that in the scheme and hustle and bustle of raising kids and work—
>
> *Jaheem*: It kind of falls by the wayside a little bit, because you have to focus on living, and then that kind of takes a back seat until you—I hate to say it—until you need it, you know what I mean? But you have to live in order to [laughs] take care of that. And then it's prioritizing. And I hate to say it, that sounds bad, but sometimes your credit kind of falls under caring for your family and your car. I know that sounds bad, but that's how—it's prioritized.

It's not surprising that for families who are living under financial strain, making payments on credit cards and other loans often becomes relegated to a lower priority. Over time, late payments and overuse of credit takes a toll on their credit scores. Given the economy in the recent past, many respondents had experienced hardships such as layoffs and prolonged unemployment and used credit to make ends meet.

Many homebuyers felt stuck and frustrated by their bad credit. For instance, Ava, 38, elaborated:

> Well, my credit score really hasn't moved much, so at this point I don't know what my options are because lenders, they'll tell you a little bit like, "Oh, you need to improve your credit," and you're like, "Okay. And then what?" Like, well, how do I do that? Especially if I have things I can't really dispute. I did make those late payments, and if they were within the seven years, they're not coming off [laughs]. I was like, I've got to wait seven years to get a house?

Like Ava, some respondents found the process of improving a bad credit score opaque, long, and difficult to navigate. Homebuyers felt that they were ready for the responsibility of homeownership and that their hard work should earn them the middle-class lifestyle associated with the American Dream. Credit history meant that the challenges and choices of their earlier lives followed them long after they thought they had moved on. Part of their frustration with credit history is the fact that it seemed not to allow them to fully become their more mature and successful adult selves.

The increased importance of higher levels of education for attaining middle-class status contributed to the credit problems that were commonplace among these homebuyers. In many cases, student loans were the source of homebuyers' credit problems. Natalie, a 35-year-old teacher's assistant, shared that when she was laid off for a time, she had trouble paying her bills:

> [The] light bill, gas bill, student loans, I mean, school bills, because my financial aid ran out, so that made me end up having to drop out of school until I got the money to pay the balance. [And then] my financial aid ran out because I ended up having to drop out of school a few times when my kids were small because they were sick. And no one let me know, like, don't keep dropping out. Because when you do that, you're messing up your financial aid, so I never knew that.

In this case, a combination of problems had led Natalie to fall into more debt than she could afford. First, she had been laid off from her work. She had also attempted to go to school while working and raising young children. Due to all of the other constraints on her time, her academic career was intermittent, and this caused her to lose her financial aid and rely more heavily on student loans. Other respondents mentioned having multiple student loans from different lenders because they had gone back to school multiple times and fell behind on payments simply because they had lost track or forgotten about some loans.

Sometimes the problem is not bad credit but lack of credit history. For instance, Emma had been living with her parents in order to save money to buy a home for herself and her son. She thought that one downside of this choice was that it may have contributed to her lack of credit history. It is possible that she would have built a longer credit history if she had been maintaining her own household. Emma explained:

> I don't pay rent, but I'm finding that that's kind of hobbling me in my house search because now I don't have any steady bills, and so with me just now getting my first credit card like two months ago, it's making me look uncreditworthy.

Many respondents found the need for a credit history surprising and confusing. There was a sense that you need credit cards and loans in order to build a history, but they can also ruin your credit if you are not careful. To some respondents, this situation seemed unfair and difficult to manage.

These examples of credit issues may seem to support the notion that irresponsible borrowers contributed to the housing crisis, but this story obscures the fact that the weak welfare state in the United States leaves many families with no choice but to turn to credit cards when they have an emergency. Monica Prasad (2012) found that the deregulation of credit markets in the United States allowed Americans to use credit to purchase services that would be provided by the welfare state in other countries with more robust welfare programs. In particular, health care costs have grown substantially in the United States, and in many cases households use credit to pay for these mounting costs. Since African Americans have relatively lower amounts of wealth, they are more exposed to this problem. Also, many homebuyers had debt from student loans, which is typically considered to be a good kind of debt in that it is debt incurred for the purpose of investment. In general, a higher percentage of Black households carry student loan debt, compared to White households (Dettling et al. 2017).

While higher education is usually a worthwhile investment, the variance in returns to a college degree has grown. There are lower returns for degrees in certain majors or degrees from for-profit colleges (Avery and Turner 2012). Nidia Bañuelos (2019) argues that for-profit colleges have benefited from a shift towards rhetorically describing education as a consumer good, at the expense of students who are not in a position to evaluate educational opportunities the same way they can evaluate other consumer goods. As higher education regulations are loosened, and the influence of the college-as-product metaphor spreads, there are more bad options available to students that can then lead to dire financial situations. Also, paying for college can be an especially bad investment if the student is unable to complete his or her degree. Under these circumstances, students can find it difficult to assess whether they are taking on an appropriate amount of debt for their situation. Furthermore, student loans are particularly difficult to discharge in bankruptcy, making them especially damaging if they do not result in higher earnings. Finally, many homebuyers lacked credit history, which is distinct from having a bad credit history. In wealthier families, people can actually inherit good credit history (for instance, a parent can boost their adult child's credit score by giving them a credit card on their own account). Without this kind of support and knowledge of the credit system, individuals frequently find it difficult to build a good credit history.

Since credit scores are typically the biggest obstacle to homeownership among this group of homebuyers, the Neighborhood Housing Services (NHS) and West Cook Homeownership Center housing counselors spend a lot of time educating prospective homebuyers on this topic. It takes up a large portion of the curriculum at Home Buyer Education courses, and class attendees ask many questions about the topic. Homebuyers mention often that they have gone to housing counselors primarily to get advice on improving their credit. One woman with a high credit score, Danielle, a 46-year-old Chicago Public Schools teacher, had met one-on-one with a housing counselor at NHS:

> She was fine. I think she's used to people who have like really, really bad credit, and so when she saw mine [...] she was like "Oh, okay," and it was kind of like a surprise. Because usually when people come to programs like that, it's because they have bad credit, and my situation is I don't have bad credit, but I just didn't have the money. I don't have a lot of debt. I don't have a down payment.

Danielle's experience demonstrates that having good credit is necessary but not sufficient for buying a home. In her case, she had a good credit score, but another issue stood in her way—she still had not accumulated the wealth necessary to purchase a home.

Decoupling School and Home Choice

One major factor that changed for homebuyers who were delayed in their home purchase process was whether or not schools were part of their search. Many homebuyers had older children who had already left home. Some had children who were older but still school-age and did not want to disrupt them by moving them to a different school. Annette Lareau and Kimberly Goyette (2014) have addressed how home choices and school choices are often made together. But the ability to use home choice to access good schools is often a privilege reserved for the most well-resourced families. Maximilian Cuddy, Maria Krysan, and Amanda Lewis (2020) found that working-class families mostly choose homes without considering schools or with schools as just one factor among many in their decision-making process, because their housing choices are already so complex and constrained.

On the other hand, new public education policies, such as the creation of charter schools, which children from different neighborhoods can attend, provide more opportunities for decoupling school choice from residence in some cases. According to Mary Pattillo, Lori Delale-O'Connor, and Felicia Butts (2014), however, these programs have not adequately addressed the problem of inequality in education because the arduous school choice process presents many hurdles to disadvantaged families attempting to access quality schools. Still, many of the homebuyers in this study matched the profile of the parents in the Pattillo et al. study who sent their children to a charter school as opposed to the parents who sent their children to a neighborhood school. The authors found that in comparison to neighborhood school parents, charter school parents had higher incomes (although they were still low-income on average) and were more likely to have access to the internet, belong to a church, and have a car. Since the parents in this study were similar to the charter school parents in their study, it is not surprising that many of the parents in this study were able to navigate the complex charter school application process. Other parents in this study were able to send their children to selective enrollment schools, which have the additional hurdle of competitive entrance exams.

When homebuyers waited to buy a home until their children were already well into their school years, they had to find alternative strategies to obtain access to good schools. For instance, Hannah was looking in middle-class, outlying city neighborhoods such as Beverly and Morgan Park. She explained that schools are not a major factor in her decision because she is already happy with the schools her children attend, and they can continue at those schools as long as they live in Chicago:

> It just really has to be Chicago, because I work for Chicago Public Schools. And our children are already enrolled in—my oldest daughter goes to Lindblom, the selective enrollment [school], so I'm not looking for some place for [...] when she's already in a good school. So, we can live wherever we want to because she doesn't have to live in their attendance area because it's a selective enrollment school; and then my other two children go to school where I work, so that's not a big motivator for us, like looking for a school district. It's going to be a neighborhood that fits, a house that fits, and [...] because like I said, the school is not a factor. We don't plan on having any more children.

While Hannah was not using schools to narrow her options, she was restricted in her search because a city government employee is required to live somewhere in the city of Chicago. If she had more freedom to look at suburban districts, she may have considered other schools. Still, like Hannah, many homebuyers valued stability for their children, so they felt that it was best to keep children at their current school as long as they deemed it adequate.

Parents in Chicago have a variety of options available to them for schools that are not directly tied to residence, including charter and selective enrollment schools. For example, at the time of our first interview, Yolanda was forty-five, married, and had four children still living at home aged eighteen, eleven, ten, and eight. Her youngest three children attend a charter school in the city, and her eighteen-year-old son was about to graduate from a selective enrollment high school. Yolanda explained that she had previously sent her children to a Catholic school. She tried sending one child to the charter and decided it was better than the Catholic school, so she transferred all of her younger children to the charter school. She explained:

> I so love this school. Better than the Catholic school. I think their communications with the parents are great. They're very informal, so I really like this school. I haven't had this much knowledge from any school that my kids have attended as far as education-wise, because most of the schools they'll say, "Oh, okay, they're doing this, they're doing that." But they're not—they don't keep in contact with the parent. The schools were not informing us, like, oh, my son is not doing well in this subject. You don't just get a phone call. If you have any situation, it's open door policy. You can always come in. You can always sit in on a classroom, interview, observe. So I love—I'm big on communication. Me and my husband are very big on communication with the school. So we didn't have that opportunity at some of the Catholic schools. They didn't let you come into the classroom unless you had a scheduled appointment and I'm paying for my child's education, so I shouldn't have to be scheduling to come and see and observe what's actually happening in the classroom. So, yeah, this school is really big on—it's like they have nothing to hide.

Yolanda has access to a wide variety of schools that are not directly tied to her residence. While Catholic schools can be a useful option for parents who wish to decouple school choice from residence, these schools have a very particular set of values and practices. Not all parents prefer this style of schooling. Charter schools and selective enrollment schools provide a greater variety of types of educational environment that are decoupled from residence. All of these schooling options allowed Yolanda to avoid the neighborhood public school that would be assigned to her children based strictly on the location of their home.

Interestingly, many parents were happy with selective enrollment or charter schools in the city and felt more confident about those than schools in the suburban areas. Many of the suburban towns where these homebuyers were looking to buy homes have struggled financially in recent years, and some have underperforming schools. Some parents like Yolanda were interested in moving to a suburb for what they perceived as a safer and more family-oriented environment, but were concerned about changing their children's schools. Yolanda explained why she did not want to transfer her children to a suburban school district: "I'm not big on trying to take my kids away from something that they've gotten so used to." She felt that the suburban schools would be good, but she worried about risking any disruption when her children were in an educational environment that appeared to be working.

Some homebuyers mentioned that other parents use address falsification as a strategy to decouple school and home choice. It is widely known that many parents gain admission for their children to public schools in other districts by using a different address. Sometimes the address of another family member or a work address. The *Chicago Tribune* has reported on this phenomenon and the punitive actions that Chicago Public Schools has taken to deter parents from this practice (Perez 2016). Interestingly, the homebuyers in this study knew of cases where children who lived in the suburbs were attending city schools, which is the opposite direction one might assume this fraud would take. I think there are two possible explanations for suburban families sending children to city schools. First, many of the predominately Black or racially transitioning suburbs to the south and west of Chicago are underresourced. In some cases, their schools are struggling because White flight, population loss, and retail redlining have damaged their tax base. Second, when parents buy homes later in life, their children are already settled in schools. Parents who are interested in buying a home in a different district often do not want to disrupt their children's education by switching their school.

Multigenerational Families and Residential Relocation

Many aspects of family life have changed since Rossi conducted his study in the 1950s, and I found that the homebuying process for working-class African Americans today is shaped by these changes. There are many more single-parent-headed households (Pew Research Center 2015) and more single-person households (Vespa, Lewis, and Kreider 2013). For African American families, a variety of household structures are common that are not captured by the traditional view of family life cycles represented in residential mobility literature. Multigenerational households have increased among all racial groups in recent years, but they continue to be more common among non-White households. The Pew Research Center defines multigenerational households in three different types: two generations (parents and adult children over age twenty-five); three generations (parents, adult children, and grandchildren); and skipped generation (grandparents and grandchildren without their parents). In a 2012 survey, Pew found that 25% of the Black population lived in a multigenerational household, compared to 14% of the White population (Taylor et al. 2010). Fifteen percent of African American children lived with a grandparent compared to seven percent of White children (Livingston 2013). Thomas Shapiro (2004) claims that African Americans often use moving in with extended family as a strategy to save resources for eventually purchasing a home. This strategy is employed as an alternative in situations where families with greater wealth often receive monetary assistance from their relatives.

The Housing Needs of Diverse Household Forms

The homebuyers in this study had varied needs due to the variety of their household forms, including single adults, married couples, married couples with children, and multigenerational households. In the case of multigenerational households, needs were associated with multiple parts of the traditional housing life cycle. Some of the aspiring homebuyers felt driven to become homeowners to signal their responsible, adult status, despite the fact that they did not have children or spouses. For instance, Amira, 31, had decided to look for a home to buy on her own. I asked her when and why she began considering buying a home:

> Actually, when I moved in with my roommate, it was because I wanted to move and I was thinking about buying at the time, and I actually had just started—I started in real estate probably a couple years before that. He was looking for a roommate so I was actually hired by him to get him roommates but it was just so cheap. I was like oh, I can move in for six months and buy, and I stayed for five years (laughs) because it was so cheap. Yeah, so this time around when I'm actually looking for things, really started probably November or October of last year because I was just at a point where, you know, it was time for me to move. I had cheap rent for a really long time, it was time for me to grow up if you will.

As I discussed in Chapter 2, many of the homebuyers felt that homeownership represented adult status and independence. For this reason, Amira felt a need to buy a home, although she does not have a partner or children to share the space of a home with her. In order to meet her needs as a single person, she will be looking mostly at condominiums.

Some homebuyers were considering the needs of older relatives who may eventually need to move in with them. Ruth, who was living with her aging parents, had to consider how their needs might grow in the near future as she looked to buy a home for the first time. Ruth explained:

> My grandmother lived to be ninety-one. They're the long-livers on that side, so it's already been understood that when I do get a home, that eventually we've already had the conversation that if something was to happen to either one of them, whichever one, the other one would come and stay with me.

Ruth was looking at particular styles of homes and particular suburbs in order to accommodate needs that she anticipated for herself and her parents. She discussed these concerns with her parents as she was looking for a home:

> Now, my dad [says]—"You don't need a house with a backyard. You don't need all those." I said, well, [laughs]—and now, since I'm kind of being bitten with the knee problem or whatever, I'm kind of paying good attention, close attention to like a lot of stairs, because some of these homes out there, like especially in like in Matteson and Richland Park, the newer homes are beautiful, but they have like these—I don't know if you're old enough to remember Dynasty [the 1980s television show]. [On] Dynasty, [the houses had] free-flowing stairs and everything else like that. I'm like, the house is beautiful, but I don't want to pass out [laughs] coming up and down the stairs. So that's why Crete and Steger have been kind of a little exciting, a little bit more attractive to me because they have a lot of homes that are ranch style.

Many first-time homebuyers in this study were older or had older relatives to consider. In some cases, households with grandparents had to consider the needs of older family members (manageable stairs) and children (quality schools). Balancing all of these different needs for family members of different ages was a significant challenge for homebuyers.

Some older homebuyers were also considering the needs of their grandchildren, who may move in and out of their household. For instance, Barbara, who was in her fifties, was taking into account the needs of her adult daughter and her fourteen-year-old granddaughter. When I asked what was most important to her in choosing a home, she replied, "The location, the schools. When we say location, we're looking at schools and churches and all that stuff." Also, her granddaughter was a major factor in her wanting to become a homeowner again after having experienced a foreclosure. Barbara explained:

> My daughter sort of like brought it up to me, and we started thinking about it, and we decided that we would try to purchase a home, so my granddaughter could live in a home, and she could see the difference as well. Because I remember we were working on our credit report in 2012, I think it was. And then this year we just got a little bit more serious about it, because we wanted our granddaughter to be in a home and try to get her situated where she's going to be.

Barbara wanted her granddaughter to have a stable living situation before she began high school. As I mentioned in Chapter 2, many homebuyers used the term "home" to refer exclusively to a single-family, detached, owner-occupied house. At the time of our first interview, Barbara's family was currently renting an apartment in a middle-class, predominately White suburb with well-regarded schools. Barbara's granddaughter had attended school in that suburban district intermittently throughout her childhood, and at other times had lived with her father on the West Side of the city and attended school there. Barbara was pleased with this suburban town and the schools there, but she felt that it was important to provide her granddaughter with the lifestyle that comes with owning a home rather than living in a rental apartment. She believes that this kind of dwelling is the best setting to raise a child and that raising children in a house socializes them to particular norms.

This belief—that being raised in a "home" helps to properly socialize individuals into middle-class norms—is also evident in the way that homebuyers talk about former public housing residents, as I discussed in Chapter 2. Homebuyers believe that lack of experience of living in "homes" is the underlying cause for the difference in culture and practice that they see between themselves and former public housing residents. Therefore, Barbara is concerned that her granddaughter may grow up without the socializing experience of living in a "home" unless she and her daughter are able to purchase one quickly. Thus, what might strike an outsider as the best choice for her daughter—remaining in a suburb with highly regarded schools even if she has to rent—is not an obvious choice to Barbara. Rather, Barbara was concerned about the schools in some of the western suburbs where they could afford to buy a home. She was considering purchasing a home in Maywood, a suburb where they had lived previously that has experienced White flight in the last few decades. She generally likes the area but feels that the neighborhood high schools have declined in quality. She hopes that her granddaughter will be accepted into a competitive math and science magnet school. If her daughter is accepted to the magnet school, they can buy a home in this relatively more affordable area without sacrificing the quality of her education. Still, Barbara is considering compromising on school quality in order to give her granddaughter the experience of living in a "home" because Barbara also considers this important for her development and the maintenance of her middle-class status.

Multigenerational Households as a Resource

Many homebuyers moved in with family for long periods while they waited to find the right property or prepared themselves financially to buy a home. For instance, Michelle wanted to buy her own home after her divorce, and she moved in with her parents in order to be in a better position to buy:

> My landlord was offering of course to extend my lease, but I still felt like I could find something. I didn't want to get tied into another one-year lease, so I put everything in storage, moved in here with my parents. And I've been here ever since [September 2014], because when I kept finding places and the same thing is happening. A lot of the foreclosed properties, they want cash. I don't have cash, so even though I may be able to get approved for certain amounts, these properties that are in foreclosure, they want fast money.

Michelle could afford a mortgage that would cover the cost of the foreclosed properties in the areas where she wanted to buy, but these properties often sold quickly to investors who were able to pay in cash. While she waited for an available property in her price range that met her needs, it was easier to live with family than to take on a lease that she might have to break.

Michelle moved in with her parents in September of 2014 with her infant grandchild and her own eleven-year-old son. It took almost exactly a year for her to buy a home. Because Michelle moved in with her parents after the 2014–15 school year had started, she was able to keep her son in the school he was already attending in Oak Park, where they had been renting an apartment. To note, Michelle was particularly concerned about school quality because her son is a special needs student. Michelle felt that the Oak Park school district (which is widely well regarded) was far superior to the one for her parents' home. Her parents still lived in the neighborhood where she grew up, which she felt had deteriorated in recent years. By the fall of 2015, though, Michelle was still not able to buy a home in Oak Park, and she felt that she could not afford to wait any longer and risk sending her son to a poor-quality school. As a result, she made a purchase in another suburb in time for the 2015–16 school year. Moving in with family can be a useful strategy for preparing to buy a home, but it brings with it a variety of risks and costs. In particular, for parents of school-age children, waiting just a year to buy into a good school district is a considerable cost.

While some aspiring homebuyers moved in with family to prepare themselves for a home purchase, other homebuyers delayed their own home purchase in order to assist older relatives. Scott, a 41-year-old married father of four, explained that he was tired of living in his parents' home, which he had moved into in order to assist his parents financially:

> I really don't like it. Honestly, it's a really nice home, don't get me wrong, it's very nice, but it's not what I would buy and spend thirty years in, you know what I mean? It doesn't have an open floor plan like I like. There's no island. There's none of that. But this was a process to help my parents. That's what this was, so we took over in '06, kind of got stuck. [Laughs] I got stuck there for a little while, but it is what it is.

Scott began renting this house from his parents in 2006 in order to help his parents, who had been mired in a challenging financial situation. Scott was not actually living in a multigenerational household because his parents lived elsewhere, but it was similar in that multiple generations were involved in this housing arrangement. Even though he had intended for the move to be a temporary solution, at the time of our interview, Scott had been there for nine years.

In addition to Scott's frustrations with the home itself, he did not feel that it was located in the best place to raise children. He explained:

> Well, of course, we have children, and we definitely want a safer environment for the children, so that's one of the key reasons of looking to move out further in the burbs somewhere. But other than that, it's just—city life after a while, it becomes—it's for the youngins, is what they call it. It's for the younger people, when you want to be in the mix, and in the know, and in and around town. And I've outgrown—my wife and I both actually have outgrown it, so it's time to move on. Plus, we want something safe for the kids, yeah.

In March of 2015 when I interviewed Scott, he had three children living at home, aged thirteen, eleven, and nine. He also had one eighteen-year-old daughter who had already left home for college. When Scott moved into his parents' home for what he had hoped would be a short stay, he had had a newborn baby and children aged nine, four, and two. Scott would have preferred to move to a safer environment for his children nine years earlier, but his family's circumstances did not allow him to make that move. As a result of that time lag, his oldest will not be able to benefit at all from a move to an improved neighborhood context. In Scott's case though, he still has younger school-age children, so his desire for the new home has not changed substantially.

While some aspiring homebuyers like Scott waited to buy homes in order to assist older relatives financially, others put their own ambitions on hold in order to provide care for older relatives. For example, Ruth moved into her parents' home to help them care for her elderly grandmother. She explained how she nearly bought a home in 2011, but she put the process on hold so she could assist her relatives:

> So, at the end of 2011, because I initially started into the contract in 2009—excuse me, 2011—at the end of the contract, I did not further pursue it because the housing market was really going really bad, and one of the issues was the selling price that the owner wanted. [...] They were not going to—the appraisers were not going to appraise it for the price that he wanted to sell it. And at that time, my mother had since then taken in my grandmother, who was suffering from dementia, Alzheimer's, an alphabet soup of what goes with getting older, and my mother was the only living child. So I moved back in with my mother and father to help my mother with my grandmother, so that's it. So, I've been back, moved back in, and I've been back there since 2011.

I conducted an initial interview with Ruth in February of 2015, four years after she had moved back in with her parents. Even in 2011, at the age of forty-three, Ruth would have been older than average for a first-time homebuyer, since the median age for a first-time homebuyer is around thirty in the United States (Bleemer et al. 2014). There were two parallel reasons why Ruth did not buy a home in 2011. First, she faced challenges navigating the housing market. Second, her grandmother was ill, and the family was able to help one another during a difficult time by creating a three-generation household. Ruth explains her decision to remain in a multigenerational household and delay her own home purchase with a blend of altruistic and personal necessity-based reasons. Multigenerational households are a tool that families can use to pool their resources. In this way, they can be both a burden and an asset for different family members at different times. For homebuyers like Ruth, the multigenerational household has been both an aid and a responsibility. At times, it can be difficult to disentangle these aspects because it is not always the case that one generation is the clear benefactor. Often, the multigenerational arrangement is helping everyone involved cope with limited resources. Also, if Ruth had greater financial assets, she could help her extended family by giving them money. Without greater savings to draw on, Ruth felt compelled to make residential relocation choices that would allow her to share resources with extended family.

Complexities of Relocating Multigenerational Households

Since homebuyers often lived with many different types of multigenerational family arrangements, decisions about homebuying often had to be made in the context of decisions about family arrangements. Keshia was 28 and lived in an apartment in Englewood with her father and her two young sons. She is looking to buy a single-family home in a south suburb instead. Her ex-husband and father of her children lives in South Holland, Illinois, so they are looking at that community or something close by. I asked her about who would be moving to their new home:

Interviewer: Would you be expecting your father to come with you or—

Keshia: We talked about it, but I don't know. Yeah… He said I think we should get a house together. I'm like, okay [laughs].

Interviewer: So, what do you think about that possibility?

Keshia: It's from what he says, like it'll be helping me out, like as far as he'll be half and half on everything. But I'm like I'm kind of grown, but I understand what he's saying, like he can help me.

In this case, Keshia's desire to become a homeowner has created a moment to reconsider her familial living arrangement. Buying a home with her father would make their current arrangement more permanent. Although this arrangement has many practical benefits for Keshia, she likes the idea of a more independent lifestyle. As I discuss in Chapter 2, owning one's own home can be symbolic of adult status and personal freedom. For homebuyers like Keshia, the home purchase process included decision making and negotiations about the composition of the new household.

Other homebuyers had ambivalence and uncertainty about their household but were planning to go forward with a home purchase regardless. For instance, Holly, 27, also aimed to buy a home so that she could have more space for herself and her six-year-old son (now that her son lives with her full-time). Furthermore, she mentioned that she may want to have another child and eventually may want to live with her boyfriend of three years:

Interviewer: So, it's just you and your son now, and do you expect that to be the same in the new place?

Holly: I do want to have another baby, so once I get my house and when I get myself comfortable, then I'll think about having another child. So maybe within a year of staying there I might get pregnant. I don't know [laughs].

Interviewer: All right, and but you mentioned a boyfriend of three years. You don't expect him to move into the next place or—

Holly: We're talking about moving in. We're talking about moving in, so that's a possibility. He might come stay with me, but—or I might go stay with—it depends. If I go stay with him then I could probably rent my house out or I don't know. We'll work it out [laughs].

So, Holly's family is very much in flux at the same time she wants to settle down in a more permanent home. While her household technically consists of just herself and her son, her mother and her long-term boyfriend are significant factors as she decides what type of home she wants and where she wants to locate. In the past, Holly's son has gone back and forth between living with her and her mother. Holly mentioned that her son is very close to her mother because "she used to help out a whole lot." This multigenerational arrangement was clearly an important resource for Holly that made it easier for her to be a successful single parent.

On the other hand, delaying the start of her own independent household for Holly and her son has created emotional entanglements that are making it more difficult for her to move on her own now. When Holly had a place in DeKalb, "[her son] used to get homesick if we were there too long, and whine and cry about her." Holly mentioned that if it were not for her need to be close to her mother, she would consider places farther out in the suburbs. Also, the apartment that she currently rents is just a few blocks away from her boyfriend's apartment. These different possible family arrangements—living on her own, with her boyfriend, or her mother—were major considerations as she made decisions about when and where to buy a home. Holly and other homebuyers in similar situations could not take for granted a traditional, linear set of household changes. In cases like this, the desire to become a homeowner outweighed the uncertainty around family arrangements. Some homebuyers like Holly felt that it would be easier to buy a home and deal with household changes after the fact.

The cross-generational support enabled by multigenerational households is an important resource. It serves as a safety net for many families as it allows them to pool their resources and provide each other with in-kind assistance. In particular, multigenerational households can help grandparents provide invaluable assistance to their single-parent adult children. On the other hand, multigenerational households also make the process of residential relocation more complicated. Households with multiple generations at different life stages have a greater diversity of needs that must be accommodated with a single housing choice. Furthermore, they include more decision makers who must come to an agreement, not just about relocation choices, but also about the makeup of the household.

Conclusion

Much of what Rossi wrote about families' residential relocation is true for middle-income African American households today. Households change over time as they grow and age. Households look to move when their current dwellings no longer meet the needs of their household type, age, and size. A few factors complicate this process for the middle-income African American households in this study. First, many had to wait a long time between when they first assessed a need for a new type of home and actually being able to move into a new home. During that time, the composition of the household often changed, and as a result, the needs of the household changed. Additionally, many of these households were multigenerational. Relocation was more complicated for multigenerational households because they had a wider variety of needs and concerns. Furthermore, the composition of the household was not a stable entity. Often, who would make up the new household was a topic that needed to be decided as part of the relocation process.

On the one hand, multigenerational living arrangements were used as a tool for preparing to purchase a home. By combining households, household members could save and pool their resources to make homeownership attainable. On the other hand, the importance placed on homeownership as independence made many disparage the idea of living in multigenerational homes long-term. Homebuyers who were otherwise comfortable living in homes owned by relatives wanted to buy their own homes in order to achieve the socially desirable status of homeowner. Because homeownership is associated with adult status, independence, and moral worth, it is viewed as an important step in the life course.

Concerns about schools were an important factor that changed over the life course of families. Families need access to quality schools for a relatively short period of time. It was often not possible for a household to time their purchase of home according to when they needed access to schools. Therefore, many households had sought out ways to decouple school from home choice. Many parents sought out charter schools and selective enrollment schools as options they could access that are not directly tied to residence. Interestingly, parents were often already sending their children to charter and selective enrollment schools in the city that they preferred over some suburban schools. Parents were aware that many suburban schools in more distressed suburbs are suffering and were generally reluctant to change their children's schools. As a result, educational concerns actually lowered the appeal of some suburbs. Still, many homebuyers were interested in suburbs for other amenities that they offer (larger homes, low crime, and retail options, for example). Although there were decoupling strategies available to families, accessing quality schools was a considerable hardship and frustration for some families. Also, grandparents living in multigenerational households were considering schools and household needs associated with aging at the same time.

Poor credit history—essentially the result of debt or negative wealth—was the main source of delay in homebuying. Aspiring homebuyers saw themselves as responsible, hardworking, middle-class adults who were ready to take the next step towards achieving the American Dream. Poor credit histories are the result of not having a wealth safety net (either a personal or a familial one) because debt must be used to handle any economic hardship that cannot be covered by regular income. For these aspiring homebuyers, poor credit histories also represented the problems of their past haunting their futures. Through educational and work achievements, they were ready for homeownership, which is viewed as a morally important status. Yet they felt deep frustration over credit histories that still reflected the challenges they had faced and choices they had made at an earlier stage in their life. The structure of credit scores makes it difficult to move past the situations of their youth.

In sum, the temporality of residential relocation decisions further complicates the homebuying process for Black families. Households that experience a delay in homebuying find it more difficult to access quality schools through home choice. They have fewer years in which they can build wealth through homeownership. In some cases, homebuyers who have already started families may find it more difficult to relocate to an ideal neighborhood as their children age and have more connections with their existing residence. Finally, those homebuyers who have stayed with their families of origin while preparing to purchase their own home develop a complex set of relationships and obligations related to their multigenerational household. In this way, the multigenerational household is both a resource for families preparing for homeownership and a household characteristic that can complicate the homebuying process.

References

Avery, Christopher, and Sarah Turner. 2012. "Student Loans: Do College Students Borrow Too Much—Or Not Enough?" *Journal of Economic Perspectives* 26(1): 165–192.

Bañuelos, Nidia. 2019. "Dangerous Metaphors: The Consequences of Treating Higher Education like a Consumer Good." *Change: The Magazine of Higher Learning* 51(1): 14–21. https://doi.org/10.1080/00091383.2019.1547064.

Bleemer, Zachary, Meta Brown, Donghoon Lee, and Wilbert van der Klaauw. 2014. "Debt, Jobs, or Housing: What's Keeping Millennials at Home?" Staff report 700, Federal Reserve Bank of New York.

Choi, Jung Hyun, Alanna McCargo, and Laurie Goodman. 2019. "Three Differences between Black and White Homeownership that Add to the Housing Wealth Gap." Urban Wire, Urban Institute. February 28, 2019. www.urban.org/urban-wire/three-differences-between-black-and-white-homeownership-add-housing-wealth-gap.

Cuddy, Maximilian, Maria Krysan, and Amanda Lewis. 2020. "Choosing Homes without Choosing Schools? How Urban Parents Navigate Decisions about Neighborhoods and School Choice." *Journal of Urban Affairs* 42(8): 1180–1201. https://doi.org/10.1080/07352166.2020.1739537.

Denton, Nancy A. 2001. "Housing as a Means of Asset Accumulation: A Good Strategy for the Poor?" In *Assets for the Poor: The Benefits of Spreading Asset Ownership*, edited by T. M. Shapiro and E. N. Wolff. New York: Russell Sage Foundation.

Dettling, Lisa J., Joanne W. Hsu, Lindsay Jacobs, Kevin B. Moore, and Jeffrey P. Thompson. 2017. "Recent Trends in Wealth-Holding by Race and Ethnicity: Evidence from the Survey of Consumer Finances." Washington, D.C.: Board of Governors of the Federal Reserve System.

Lareau, Annette, and Kimberly Goyette. 2014. *Choosing Homes, Choosing Schools*. New York: Russell Sage Foundation.

Livingston, Gretchen. 2013. "At Grandmother's House We Stay: One-in-Ten Children Are Living with a Grandparent." Washington, D.C.: Pew Research Center.

Pattillo, Mary, Lori Delale-O'Connor, and Felicia Butts. 2014. "High Stakes Choosing." In *Choosing Homes, Choosing Schools*, edited by A. Lareau and K. Goyette. New York: Russell Sage Foundation.

Perez, Juan, Jr. 2016. "Fraud, Theft and 'Three Stooges' DVD Part of CPS Annual Watchdog Report." Chicago Tribune, January 4, 2016. www.chicagotribune.com/news/breaking/ct-chicago-schools-inspector-general-report-0104-20160103-story.html

Pew Research Center. 2015. "Parenting in America: Outlook, Worries, Aspirations are Strongly Linked to Financial Situation." Washington, D.C.: Pew Research Center.

Prasad, Monica. 2012. *The Land of Too Much: American Abundance and the Paradox of Poverty*. Cambridge: Harvard University Press.

Rossi, Peter H. 1980. *Why Families Move*, 2nd edition. Beverly Hills: Sage.

Shapiro, Thomas M. 2004. *The Hidden Cost of Being African American: How Wealth Perpetuates Inequality*. New York: Oxford University Press.

———. 2006. "Race, Homeownership and Wealth." *Washington University Journal of Law & Policy* 20: 53–74.

Taylor, Paul, Jeffrey Passel, Richard Fry, Richard Morin, Wendy Wang, Gabriel Velasco, and Daniel Dockterman. 2010. "The Return of the Multi-Generational Family Household." Washington, D.C.: Pew Research Center.

Vespa, Jonathan, Jamie M. Lewis, and Rose M. Kreider. 2013. "America's Families and Living Arrangements: 2012." Report P20-570. Washington, D.C.: US Census Bureau.

Zavisca, Jane. 2013. "A Home Not One's Own: How Young Russians Living with Extended Family Navigate and Negotiate Space." In *Home: International Perspectives on Culture, Identity, and Belonging*, edited by M. Kusenbach and K. E. Paulsen. Frankfurt: Peter Lang GmbH, Internationaler Verlag der Wissenschaften.

4

SEARCHING FOR A DREAM HOME

William and Gloria, who are now in their sixties, met at their high school in Chatham, a predominately Black neighborhood on the South Side of Chicago. They got married shortly after Gloria graduated from high school. Because William was in the military, they moved several times before settling in the suburb of Riverdale, Illinois just south of Chicago. Gloria had "always wanted to live in the suburbs." They had moved into the house with Gloria's parents and then taken it over after her parents passed away. When moving to Riverdale decades before, it seemed like she had achieved her goal by moving to the suburbs, but the reality was not that simple. "I always thought the suburbs was nice and quiet, something different. We were here twenty-one years, so it started out like that. It's a little different now."

William explained how homeowners, retail, and industry have left the area during that time, resulting in an atmosphere of decline that he finds similar to Detroit:

> When the businesses die and they leave, they leave massive gaps; i.e., Detroit. I was a truck driver for many years. In Detroit, I [would] take my big rig down virtually any side street, any road, because [there were] so many businesses in the communities. People live down the street from where they worked at. But when those businesses failed, when the auto industry failed, all the ancillary businesses also failed, so now you had […] deteriorating roads because the tax base wasn't there to repair it, the trucks rolling in. You had housing that now became vacant. You had businesses that were vacant. You have massive cavities all over the place. [And now], we've got blight starting to build in the very center of Riverdale. That's not going to help out. You don't see it so much in most of these houses here, but we have a lot

> of vacancy. Our neighbor next door is gone. Three houses over, that house has been vacant for about ten years.

Their experience of homeownership has been marked by neighborhood decline. Riverdale has experienced population loss and overall decline. The property tax burden has increased on the remaining homeowners while housing values have declined (the median house sales price declined 76% between 2006 and 2016). It has also experienced White flight. Riverdale went from 40% Black in 1990 to 93% Black in 2010. Gloria and William decided to leave Riverdale. They looked into buying a home elsewhere; they searched on the South Side of the city and in other south suburbs, but they were unsatisfied with their options. So, they moved in with William's parents who live in the nearby suburb of Hazel Crest. William explained, "It's not totally ideal, but it's the best port we could pull our ship into." William and Gloria found homeownership was difficult to achieve. Even when they inherited a home, that home was in a neighborhood experiencing dramatic decline and so they were unable to reap the benefits typically associated with homeownership.

Scholars of place-based disadvantage have demonstrated that racial disparities in neighborhood quality perpetuate racial inequality in the United States (Massey and Denton 1993; Sampson 2012; Sharkey 2013), but the notion of place-based disadvantage implies stable places and static people. In actuality, the average American can expect to move 11.7 times during their life, based on 2007 American Community Survey Data (US Census Bureau), and rates for lifetime moves have historically been similar for Whites and Blacks (South and Deane 1993). African Americans, like Americans generally, move often and have experienced neighborhood disadvantage compared with Whites despite their residential mobility.[1] In *Stuck in Place*, Patrick Sharkey (2013) argues that multigenerational experience of neighborhood disadvantage has driven the persistent socioeconomic disadvantage of Black families. African Americans make decisions about residential relocation in the context of this multigenerational experience of neighborhood disadvantage, which can then follow them through time and space.

Drawing on Sharkey's concept of the multigenerational experience of neighborhood decline, I argue that neighborhood disadvantage can follow geographically and socioeconomically mobile individuals over time even as they actively search for stable, racially integrated, and middle-class neighborhoods. Building on previous research on housing searches, I find that neighborhood selection can be best understood as a two-part process. Some neighborhoods are filtered out of the process before the search process even begins. While aspiring African American homebuyers understand themselves to be actively searching for stable or improving racially diverse and middle-class neighborhoods, places that might best fit these characteristics are often filtered out of their search process before they begin actively searching. Furthermore, neighborhoods that actually meet typically desired characteristics were few in number. For African Americans, moving to an integrating neighborhood can mean being part of a demographic shift towards resegregation as a changing neighborhood shifts from predominately White to Black. So, while the homebuyers in this study used what are likely to be typical housing search heuristics with the goal of stable or improving integrated neighborhoods, their searches typically resulted in segregated or resegregating neighborhoods.

Research on decision-making processes can help us to understand actual housing choices. Swait has found that in a variety of different contexts, people make choices in two different stages. The first stage of decision-making is when the choice set is formulated, while the second stage involves making a decision between potential choices. Informational, psychological, cutural, and social factors limit the number of alternatives actually considered as a part of the feasible choice set (Swait 1984; Swait and Ben-Akiva 1987; Swait and Erdem 2007). Within the imagined set of potential neighborhoods, movers apply search heuristics. Psychologists have found that when making predictions and decisions in the face of uncertainty, people often rely on a set of heuristics to make choices (Kahneman and Tversky 1973; Tversky and Kahneman 1973, 1975). Search heuristics may be an additional mechanism that can partially explain how racial segregation persists. Gerd Gigerenzer and Wolfgang Gaissmaier (2011) define a heuristic as "a strategy that ignores part of the information, with the goal of making decisions more quickly, frugally and/or accurately than more complex methods" (454). They argue that heuristics are not necessarily unreliable strategies for decision-making—how reliable they are depends upon the structure of the environment that they are intended to clarify.

Heuristics are necessary because African Americans choosing a place to buy a home within a highly racially segregated metropolitan area must contend with a great deal of uncertainty. In Chicago, researchers from the Voorhees Center for Neighborhood and Community Improvement (2014) found that neighborhoods that experienced the greatest socioeconomic decline from 1970 to 2010 were all majority African American and/or Latino, and researchers have found similar patterns elsewhere (Hwang and Sampson 2014; Jun 2016). These structural factors create an environment in which African Americans experience more neighborhood decline than Whites.

Different kinds of heuristics are used in various decision-making processes. In any kind of consumer choice, decision elimination is an important part of the process in order to limit the choice set to a reasonable number. Recognition (e.g., brand recognition) can be a useful heuristic in this kind of case. Similarly, many heuristics allow decision makers to ignore most sources of data and simplify the decision-making process by focusing on one cue or a sequence of cues (Gigerenzer and Gaissmaier 2011), or by using the first cue that surpasses a threshold deemed acceptable —known as satisficing (Simon 1987).

To study the use of heuristics, you have to observe intermediate stages in the decision-making process (Bruch and Feinberg 2017). Elizabeth Bruch, Ross

Hammond, and Peter Todd (2015) argue that "to know what heuristics to build into psychologically realistic models we must first assess the relevant features of that environment that shape decision strategies" (5). Furthermore, decisions that some movers make may change the environment in which others make their own decisions, because the choices of each mover subsequently change the composition of their destination and origin neighborhoods.

Relatedly, Michael Bader and Maria Krysan (2015) point to the importance of an existing racialized geography in contributing to future residential relocation decisions. They used a question about two suburbs—one predominately Black and the other predominately White—to demonstrate how the existing geography of racial segregation can influence preferences in a way that preserves racial segregation. For instance, Schaumburg and Homewood/Flossmoor are similar in terms of the incomes of residents and cost of homes, but Schaumburg is a predominately White suburb to the north of Chicago, and Homewood/Flossmoor is a predominately Black suburb to the south of Chicago. When asked whether they would consider Schaumburg, Black respondents said that it was isolated from schools, jobs, and family, whereas Whites gave a similar response about Homewood/Flossmoor. Similarly, Kris Marsh and Kivan Polimis (2014) find that both Black and White adults tend to live in neighborhoods with similar racial compositions to the ones they had lived in as adolescents, but this association is strongest for Whites. In other words, the existing geography of race contributes to Whites' and Blacks' differing levels of familiarity, comfort, and sense of connection to certain parts of the metropolitan area. This racialized geography informs the first order of neighborhood choices. Some neighborhoods are never under serious consideration due to their location in a racialized mental map of the city. Much of what I have found confirms what Krysan and Bader found about first-order filtering. What Krysan and Bader add is an explanation of how the combination of first- and second-order filtering under the structural conditions of hyper–racial segregation led African American homebuyers to neighborhoods that do not meet their desired characteristics.

Ideal Neighborhood Qualities

African American homebuyers generally have a clear idea of the racial demographics that would be ideal in a neighborhood, as well as other characteristics that generally make for good neighborhoods. Additionally, many homebuyers feel that they are actively searching for these neighborhoods and that they even select neighborhoods that will meet this ideal, but the combination of first-order filtering and search heuristics may actually lead homebuyers to places that fall far short of these ideal characteristics. I discuss the neighborhoods where homebuyers ended up in Chapter 6. In general, these ideal characteristics include rising housing values, respectable and polite neighbors, low crime, access to a variety of amenities, and racial diversity.

Most of the homebuyers sought to live in a racially diverse community, although this is seldom a stable state for a neighborhood. Jill, 41, aspires to live in a racially diverse community, partly because she believes this is the ideal environment in which to raise children. She explained:

> I would say [diversity is] kind of paramount in my decision-making. It's important to me because I'd like to be exposed to different races and different cultures for a different view, a different perspective. Also, I want my daughter to be exposed to a world that's just not all Black, but I also don't want her to be the only one, like the token Black kid in the area, because that's isolating.

Many respondents felt that racial diversity was a nice attribute to have in a neighborhood for their own sake but, more importantly, for properly raising children. Like many of the homebuyers, she believes that racial diversity has intrinsic value as a neighborhood quality.

These discussions of diversity were aspirational. At the outset of the study, most of the homebuyers lived in predominately Black neighborhoods. About half of the homebuyers lived in a neighborhood that was greater than 70% non-Hispanic Black. When asked to elaborate on the kind of diversity they wanted to see, they would typically bring up racial diversity; specifically, they wanted to see a greater number of non-Black neighbors, but not an entirely White neighborhood. Recent sociological investigations of diversity discourse have highlighted the ways in which this term is understood and deployed by Whites. Berrey (2015) explains how this term came into ascendency in the wake of the 1978 *Regents of the University of California v. Bakke* Supreme Court case,[2] which enshrined the educational benefits of diversity as the best defense of affirmative action in higher education. The idea that diversity should be promoted for these diffuse benefits extends to other settings. Ellen Berrey found that a number of different constituencies promoted neighborhood diversity from this stance, including corporate interests, boosters, and developers. Ultimately, those arguing in favor of fair housing also framed their policy goals in terms of the benefits of diversity for the neighborhood, rather than promoting these programs as a remedy for past wrongs or a tool to lessen racial inequality.

By contrast, this study demonstrates what diversity means as an aspirational value for working-class African Americans. For working-class Black aspiring homebuyers, neighborhood racial diversity is seen as an intrinsically valuable neighborhood quality, an indicator of other good neighborhood qualities, and a sign of general progress towards greater racial justice. With this kind of diversity, neighborhoods with a substantial number of Black and White residents can be valued without denigrating Black people or Black spaces. Homebuyers thought that interaction with people who have other perspectives was useful, and they also saw that neighborhoods with Whites get access to resources that predominately Black neighborhoods do not often get, and they thought that they had lots in common culturally with middle-class White homeowners and believed that they should be able to share residential spaces with this population comfortably. The homebuyers' perspective represents a different point of view on the value of diversity than Natasha Warikoo (2016) found among college students, particularly White college students in the US. White college students tend to frame diversity in terms of a bargain in which students of color provide an enriching environment for White students and in return they gain access to the resources of powerful institutions. In this case, Black homebuyers regarded diversity as an intrinsic good for themselves and their children. In other words, while Black homebuyers use the now ubiquitous term of diversity to describe the racially mixed neighborhoods they desire, they imbue it with a different set of meanings than some other constituencies.

The ways that the homebuyers in this study employ diversity is similar to what Sarah Mayorga-Gallo (2014) found among Black residents of a multiracial and multiethnic neighborhood in Durham—for this group, a diverse neighborhood was one with enough non-White residents to make it seem safe and comfortable for Black residents, and with enough non-Black residents to bring the cultural and economic benefits they felt were associated with racially mixed places. Interestingly, in Mayorga-Gallo's *Behind the White Picket Fence*, it does seem that Black residents were more ambivalent about the socio-cultural benefits of living in a diverse neighborhood, suggesting that the lived experience of interacting in this kind of neighborhood was more complex than what the homebuyers in this study anticipated before moving.

For those who were able to relocate to more diverse neighborhoods, it remains to be seen whether that diversity lives up to the promise of their ideal. Evelyn Perry (2016) has argued that Whites who claim to value racial diversity often act in ways that perpetuate racial inequality within racially diverse places. She points out that by virtue of bringing people together who think and act differently from each other, diverse neighborhoods are generally sites of tension and some conflict. Similarly, Jan Doering (2020) found that racially mixed, gentrifying neighborhoods can become insidious sites of racial marginalization as residents who have greater access to powerful institutions above the neighborhood level are able to wield their structural advantage in the neighborhood. Integrated neighborhoods are not inherently equitable places; the structures of racial injustice that inform our entire society shape the daily interactions throughout these spaces. This study cannot speak to the experience of actually living in such a neighborhood, as these works by Doering, Perry and Mayorga-Gallo's do. Rather, this study looks at how this ideal is understood by working-class Black aspiring homebuyers and how they go about trying to access this ideal neighborhood under structural conditions that make these neighborhoods rare and often precarious.

What Determines the Choice Set

A variety of factors limited the initial set of choices that particular homebuyers view as available, including financial resources, transportation, and employment restrictions (many employees of the city of Chicago are required to live within the city limits). Some neighborhoods are excluded from the search because they are unattainable owing to housing values or other constraints. Other neighborhoods are excluded from the search because either homebuyers have no knowledge of them or they are too far away from where they work or engage in other regular activities. These initial limits on the choice set based on geography and other factors can be considered the first-order filtering process. Bader and Krysan (2015) have demonstrated how the radicalized geography of the city influences what areas are under consideration as part of this initial choice set, and their research confirms this finding. Some neighborhoods were believed to be unwelcoming due to the racial demographics of the neighborhood or previous experiences in neighborhoods with similar racial demographics. The initial choice set often excludes neighborhoods that would allow the mover to make an integrative move. In order to understand the role of search heuristics (the active filtering process applied to the imagined choice set), we must first understand what determines the choice set.

Most homebuyers did not include neighborhoods on the north side of the city and in the northern suburbs in their choice set, which are farther from predominately Black neighborhoods and where fewer neighborhoods have experienced White flight. I asked Kaya about Schaumburg, a predominately White suburb to the north of the city where the median home value in 2014 was $240,200. Schaumburg has a small Black population (4.2% in 2010), which had increased modestly since 2000 (21.8% increase), making it seem quite likely that it will retain a large non-Black population in the near future. I thought this area seemed like a reasonable option for Kaya given the towns she was considering, which had median home values ranging from $132,900 (Country Club Hills) to $275,700 (Orland Park). The median income in Schaumburg was $72,745 in 2014, which is similar to that of Oak Forest ($71,082), slightly higher than that of Matteson ($67,170) and lower than that of Tinley Park ($75,991) (US Census Bureau 2014). Kaya replied to my question about Schaumburg:

> Well, you know, my husband just mentioned something to me about Schaumburg, too, the other day, so we haven't looked there at all yet, but probably on our list.

In a later interview, she told me that she had decided Schaumburg was too far away from all the places that are part of her family's regular routine. Like many of the homebuyers, Kaya felt pulled toward the southern and western portions of the metropolitan area because of her greater sense of familiarity with the area. While Kaya was aware of Schaumburg and it could have been a realistic option for her, this town never made it into the set of suburbs that she seriously considered. Kaya had excluded Schaumburg because of its seemingly distant location in her mental map of the metropolitan area, all of which is informed by a racialized geography.

Previous experiences of White hostility also led homebuyers to exclude particular neighborhoods or portions of the metropolitan area. For instance, about three years earlier, Samantha, 29, and her husband had actually tried moving to a majority-White suburb, La Grange, and had experienced hostile neighbors there. Samantha recounted her experiences in La Grange:

> We had so many negative situations that happened when we were living there, which are why we moved. My husband and my son were there in Jewel [a grocery store], and my son he was maybe in second grade, and I think this older White man he walked past, and he knocked my son over. It was an accident, but he knocked him over, and he just looked at him and he just kept walking, so my husband was like, "You could at least say sorry." He's like, "Oh well, if you weren't in our store—if you people didn't come out here to our store and go to your own store, then we wouldn't have these types of situations." That's just one of the scenarios.

This negative experience in La Grange made a lasting impression on Samantha, in part because her young child was present. Although Samantha did not claim that the majority of Whites in La Grange hold racist attitudes, she was not interested in risking any repeat experience of this kind of behavior for her child. Samantha's case makes it clear that our personal histories of residential mobility overtly and covertly shape our preferences about neighborhoods, and are not just due to historical memory of White hostility.

Although Samantha had these negative experiences in a place where she had previously lived, other homebuyers were dissuaded from moving to White neighborhoods owing to previous experiences visiting these areas or because stories they had heard from friends and family dissuaded them from looking to buy homes in all-White neighborhoods. Sophia, 29, described the predominately White Mount Greenwood neighborhood:

> Going through it, you can shop there, but I wouldn't want to be on a bus stop there. I've gotten rude comments, people driving past saying things to me. I had a friend try to buy a house over there. They spray painted her driveway, so they try to keep it very Irish over there would be a nice way to say it. They don't really want anybody outside of the race over there, so it's something that you don't really want to worry about, coming home to a bunch of busted windows when you just paid your life savings into a new house. So that's why I wouldn't want—it's a nice, beautiful neighborhood, no problems, the schools are nice over there, but not necessarily welcoming.

Sophia's fears of hostility in all-White neighborhoods are not based on hypothetical notions of what these areas may be like, but instead on her own experiences and from first-hand accounts from her friends. Mount Greenwood and La Grange both happen to be in the southern and western parts of a metropolitan region near neighborhoods that have transitioned from predominately White to predominately Black. Due to the geography of these particular White enclaves, their White residents are more likely to feel threatened by the possibility of their neighborhoods' changing racially and ethnically. Additionally, Black homebuyers are more likely to encounter these White neighborhoods because they are close to places where they already have ties. These working-class and lower-middle-class African Americans are encountering the most threatening White neighborhoods—these are closest to their current residence, their places of work, and their social networks—and are extrapolating from those experiences to make judgments about other areas with overwhelmingly White populations. As a result, even if overt racial hostility from White neighbors is not widespread, it can have an effect on the decision-making of African American homebuyers.

Second-Order Neighborhood Filtering with Search Heuristics

Within the imagined set of potential neighborhoods, homebuyers use heuristics to guide them in selecting neighborhoods that they hope will maintain or gain the ideal qualities that interest them. Homebuyers have three main strategies for the search process: avoiding decline; searching for improvement; and searching for stability. While nearly all homebuyers are concerned with avoiding decline, some homebuyers are more interested in stability, and others are more interested in potential improvement. When avoiding decline, homebuyers use the heuristic of avoiding neighborhoods that exhibit signs that renters, particularly housing choice voucher recipients, live in those neighborhoods. Whether homebuyers employ improvement or stability heuristics depends on whether they are focused on meeting present or future needs. Homebuyers who feel that they have the benefit of time look for areas that they believe could improve. These homebuyers use the heuristic of looking for signs of potential improvement or gentrification. Homebuyers searching for stability want places that are suitable in the moment, often to meet the current needs of their children. They want to move to places that met their desires for neighborhood demographics and amenities right now and that they think could remain stable. These homebuyers use a satisficing heuristic in which they look for neighborhoods that appear to have enough of the characteristics that they want. Both strategies may have led homebuyers to be overly optimistic about positive outcomes in the neighborhoods that they selected, but in two different directions.

Avoiding Decline

Because homebuyers are concerned that dynamics of neighborhood decline could follow them as they move to different city neighborhoods and suburbs, homebuyers

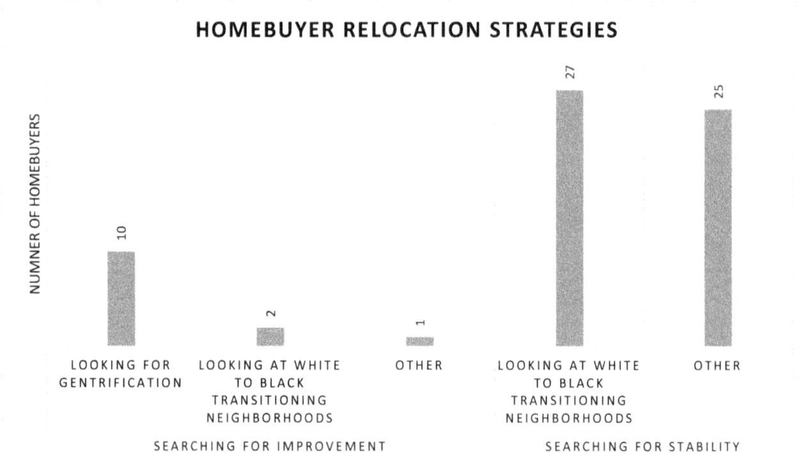

FIGURE 4.1 Homebuyer Relocation Strategies

use heuristics to evaluate the potential for neighborhood decline. The most commonly used heuristic is a belief that poorer residents who hold housing choice vouchers (HCV) cause neighborhood decline. Many of the homebuyers believe that neighborhoods declined as a consequence of the Plan for Transformation (a city-wide initiative to demolish large public housing projects and to move residents to scattered-site buildings, mixed-income developments, and the private rental market). To avoid decline, respondents try to eliminate neighborhoods from their list that they believe have high numbers of voucher holders. They look for signs that they believe indicate a presence of voucher holders or the potential for an influx of voucher holders, including behaviors of residents, maintenance of publicly visible spaces, and the total number of apartment buildings. Notably, middle-income African American homebuyers use class distinctions between Blacks as an important cue for their heuristics. While Whites involved in housing decision-making processes probably also use heuristics, research on Whites' neighborhood preferences suggests that they would be more likely to use cruder distinctions based solely on race, leading them to avoid *any* predominately Black neighborhood regardless of class distinctions. These racial distinctions are less nuanced and also easier to determine.

Homebuyers believe that subsidized renters are particularly bad neighbors and that a large presence of this population will likely cause neighborhood decline. Like many of the homebuyers, Tiffany, whom I mentioned in the introduction, believed that the suburb where she grew up has changed due to a greater proportion of renters, who she believes are former Chicago Housing Authority (CHA) residents using the HCV program:

> So, I know that a lot of the projects, the low-income housing, they tore them down: Cabrini–Green, Robert Taylor. They all moved to the south suburbs, and a lot of people started accepting Section 8, which is the old term for the program that I'm in now, which is the voucher program through CHA. And I know a lot of people want to accept it because they know that they're going to get paid immediately because of the program. A lot of people wanted to flip houses and apartments and things like that, and so it just flooded everybody that way.

Tiffany believes that the housing choice voucher recipients who moved from the large CHA housing projects—which had been torn down as part of the Plan for Transformation—are primarily responsible for the decline in Riverdale.

In the absence of large public housing towers, homebuyers like Tiffany searched for other signs of the presence of subsidized renters in a neighborhood. These signs include the physical maintenance of areas outside the home (especially lawns), use of public spaces, and quantity of younger residents (both young adults and children). Tiffany asserted that in the time since she had left home, a great deal had changed in Riverdale, including the physical appearance of homes:

> There is a certain element that kind of, in my opinion, goes along with renters versus owners. If you own, you're going to make sure there's no trash on the lawn, and you're going to roll your garbage can out to the corner so that the garbage men can pick it up, and you're going to get your mail, and you're not going to just let the newspaper sit on the front porch forever; loud music—you know to turn it down when you pull up through the driveway, just things like that. And I just noticed things were changing, and not for the better. I started seeing a lot of abandoned buildings and unmanicured lawns.

Tiffany associated certain neighborly behavioral norms with homeownership and notions of respectability, and she thought that neighborhood decline in Riverdale was the result of renters' violating these norms, which include maintaining the outward appearance of their homes. It is poignant to note that although Tiffany held a voucher herself, she hoped to leave the HCV program soon and own her home with the assistance of CHA's Choose to Own program. She proclaimed how she wanted her participation in the HCV program to be temporary—while she got on her feet and prepared to become a homeowner herself. Furthermore, she felt culturally tied to the lifestyle she had in her youth in a single-family detached home in Riverdale. In contrast, she believed that the cultural mores of former CHA residents were shaped by the large housing projects and that these norms are not compatible with those of a community of homeowners. Of course, unlike homeowners, renters are not supposed to be responsible for the maintenance of their homes because their landlords carry the primary responsibility for maintenance. Yet many of the homebuyers attributed moral significance to this difference in behavior, which stems directly from different material positions—that of a property owner versus that of a renter.

Many homebuyers see particular behaviors in outdoor spaces as signs of voucher-holder status. For example, Tabitha, 52, thought that voucher recipients use public spaces in the neighborhood inappropriately:

> I can give you a classic example. My cousin used to have a beautiful home in 81st and Blackstone, okay? Most of the people there were homeowners. Well, a lot of these landlords are taking advantage of the Section 8 vouchers. The people directly across the street from my cousin went to the house and blacktopped the front yard, set a card table and chairs out in front and put a boom box in the window. [...] A lot of people who were in the developments, they never had a yard, right? So what happens? They don't go in the backyard.

This stereotypical complaint surfaces frequently—that voucher holders use their front porches for leisure as opposed to their backyards—and this was seen as tied to the lifestyle associated with large public-housing towers. Homebuyers stridently believe that their own lifestyle choices are more appropriate for single-family homes, and a major indicator of this lifestyle is the use of the backyard for leisure.

The decentralized nature of the housing choice voucher program increases uncertainty and anxiety about the effects of subsidized renters on neighborhoods. Homebuyers associate particular behaviors with voucher holders and assume that people who exhibit those behaviors are benefiting from the voucher program. There are limited opportunities for homebuyers to have their stereotypes challenged because voucher holders who behave according to homebuyers' norms can easily go unnoticed—their behaviors do not fit predetermined expectations. Stories about Section 8 or voucher-holding tenants from Chicago moving to municipalities throughout the metro area have become commonplace, but the evidence does not suggest that many voucher recipients have in fact left the city. From 2004 to 2014, there were small increases in the number of families using housing choice vouchers in both Chicago and its suburbs. The Chicago Housing Authority had 4,194 more families using vouchers, and the Cook County Housing Authority, which serves the suburbs closest to Chicago, had an increase of 1,197 families (Center on Budget and Policy Priorities 2015). In the Chicago metropolitan area, there was actually a decline in the percentage of housing choice voucher recipients living in the suburbs (Covington, Freeman, and Stoll 2011).

Searching for Improvement

One strategy homebuyers employed for identifying higher socioeconomic status and potentially more racially diverse area at an affordable price was to look for places that could improve in the future. Younger, often single and childless homebuyers who primarily want to buy condominiums or multiunit buildings in more densely built parts of the city use this strategy. They often spoke about neighborhoods with potential for improvement as ones that could gentrify or were "up and coming." Cues that homebuyers used to indicate neighborhoods that could gentrify were indications of potential for gentrification from real estate agents and new neighborhood developments. When home prices are low enough, homebuyers are willing to gamble on buying a home in a lower-income, predominately Black area that they think will attract economic development in the near future. Although homebuyers have generally not experienced substantial White gentrification in the neighborhoods where they have lived, many believe that it is a fairly common phenomenon in Chicago.

Some real estate agents encourage this optimistic outlook on the possibility of gentrification in neighborhoods where they are showing homes. Liam explained that he is looking for a condominium in South Shore because his friends and real estate agent have suggested that it may gentrify and "the resale value would most likely go up." He mentioned that his real estate agent has given him advice on which areas are most likely to undergo gentrification. Liam, 25, claimed, "She tells me about the history of the area like Washington Park and stuff like that, as far as like if they're going into gentrification, if it's a nice area to live in." In this case, the real estate agent is selling the possibility of gentrification to make the condominiums in her area more appealing.

The potential to make money on a property is one reason to seek out areas that are gentrifying, but it is also a way to afford an area that may eventually be a more desirable place to live because of greater racial diversity or improved amenities. For instance, Emmanuel, 56, said of a neighborhood he was searching in:

> What's happening is that we're having a reverse White flight from the suburbs and the younger people, they are leaving the suburb and they're coming back to the city in droves, and the real estate companies are accommodating them by providing them with rehabbed homes.

Emmanuel lives in Hyde Park, which he appreciates because it is racially diverse, middle-class, low-crime, and rich with amenities. He currently uses a Section 8 voucher to rent in the neighborhood, and to purchase a home he would probably need to move to a less expensive area. Consequently, he is considering neighborhoods that he believes could have similar characteristics to that of Hyde Park in the future but that currently have cheaper home prices.

A second significant, if prosaic, reason that they saw gentrification in a positive light was that homebuyers associated it with neighborhoods that will someday have more, and better, amenities. Many of the homebuyers in this study discussed frustration with the lack of grocery stores, restaurants, chain stores, movie theaters, and community centers in Black neighborhoods. For instance, Alice, 49, explained:

> I have friends that are in the Bronzeville neighborhood. I think there is some beautiful property, but I'd call that area a food desert. There's no place to shop. You don't have a lot of little stores. You don't have a lot of big stores. I don't want to live in a food desert. And I do like the diverse neighborhood. I don't want to be in an area that's concentrated with one minority for the most part.

The way that Alice goes back and forth between neighborhood racial diversity and the availability of certain amenities makes it difficult to disentangle the relative importance of the two factors for her housing preferences. For instance, would a new grocery store in Bronzeville be enough to make it a desirable neighborhood? Or is there something beyond shopping options that Alice finds desirable about living in a more diverse neighborhood? The reality is that these factors are highly correlated because predominately Black Chicago neighborhoods and suburbs have a dearth of retail, particularly of the kind that will appeal to the middle class—Black or White. Retail redlining is the practice of retailers choosing locations based on the racial and ethnic composition of neighborhoods rather than economic factors (D'Rozario and Williams 2005). Evidence of this practice has been found in the Atlanta area where upper-income Black neighborhoods have less access to restaurants, grocery stores, and movie theaters than comparable White neighborhoods (Helling and Sawicki 2003), and similar dynamics appear to be affecting the Chicago region as well.

We can understand why Black homebuyers would want their neighborhoods to "improve." But what if homebuyers felt that the most viable route to such improvement is via an in-migration of Whites? First, as Maria Krysan and Reynolds Farley (2002) have found, most African Americans want to live in more racially diverse neighborhoods than they currently do. At the same time, many are still wary about becoming "pioneers"— one of a few Black households to initially move into a White neighborhood. So, it makes sense that in order to eventually live in places with greater racial diversity, African American homebuyers would seek out neighborhoods that already have largely minority populations but are expected to have an in-migration of Whites. The hope is that by buying into a Black neighborhood that could experience White in-migration in the future, a Black homebuyer would eventually live in a more diverse neighborhood that is also accepting, inclusive, and not dominated by White interests.

Certainly, there are homeowners in the United States who reside in Black neighborhoods that *are* gentrifying, and they may have different views, such as those studied by Monique Taylor (2002) and Lance Freeman (2011). And some securely middle-class African Americans may deliberately move back to Black neighborhoods, hoping in part to help stabilize or improve them, as I discussed in Chapter 2 and as shown by Mary Pattillo (2008). Some may, as Michelle Boyd (2008) has found, have a "racial nostalgia" for what they imagined to be the tightly knit Black communities of the Jim Crow era, when even upper-income African Americans had no other choice but to live in Black areas. But for most of the homebuyers in this study, choosing an all-Black neighborhood was neither attractive nor a financially wise decision. If they bought a house, their family's future would be closely tied to the fortunes of their neighborhood.

So, for these homeowners, the alluring prospects of gentrification were in no way lessened by the idea that this would involve White in-migration. They regarded gentrification as a package that would bring returns to their investment, improved neighborhood amenities, especially retail outlets, and greater racial diversity. They considered the prospect of seeking out a gentrifying neighborhood as a way to achieve these goals, but, in fact, the odds are against them. Gentrification is a fairly unusual phenomenon and the neighborhoods where they were looking are less likely to gentrify and more likely to decline. Some neighborhoods *will* gentrify—there will be relatively poor and non-White neighborhoods into which middle-class Whites move, probably bringing new amenities in their wake—but these are likely to be Hispanic neighborhoods, not ones with a substantial Black population (Anderson and Sternberg 2012).

Searching for Stability

Some of the homebuyers are looking primarily for neighborhoods that they thought would remain stable, rather than trying to seek improving neighborhoods. These homebuyers used the strategy of searching for stability in terms of neighborhood demographics, amenities, and housing values. They used a satisficing (Simon 1987) heuristic for their search, in that they looked for neighborhoods that had enough of the features that they sought. They used the lack of recent visible changes as a cue for neighborhood stability. These homebuyers tend to be a bit older and to have more children in their households. In contrast to the group that searches for improving neighborhoods, homebuyers looking for stability are mostly buying in outlying bungalow neighborhoods of Chicago (that is, residential neighborhoods with single-family detached houses) or in suburbs. The homebuyers using the stability heuristic want similar things as those using the improvement heuristic in terms of neighborhood demographics, namely more middle-class and more White neighborhoods with more amenities. The difference was that those looking for stability have a greater interest in having those neighborhood characteristics now and in maintaining them in the future. Compared to homebuyers searching for improvement, those searching for stability feel that they had less time to wait. For example, one homebuyer, Lucy, had moved to South

Shore searching for improvement but grew impatient with the lack of progress in that neighborhood and became more interested in stability for her next move.

While many of the homebuyers were looking in areas that are experiencing a great deal of change, they were often preoccupied with the ideal of stability. When I asked Bonnie, 63, what were her most important factors in choosing a home, she replied succinctly, "Neighborhood. That's important to me. Stability. How stable is it?" I asked Bonnie what she meant by stability and she explained:

> I don't like a bunch of changes, a bunch of changes like in the neighborhood. Okay, you see a whole bunch of building up stuff. It's good for changes for the better and everything, but I mean, if this is supposed to be a residential area, I want it to be a residential area. I don't want some big complex or whatever, they're starting to build and everything, and this is a stable area. Yeah.

Unlike homebuyers who were looking for improvement, for Bonnie, signs of change are something to be avoided. While Bonnie admits that some changes are good, she is generally disposed to be wary of change. In part, her disposition arises from her life stage. Bonnie is retired and lives alone. Homebuyers like Bonnie, who had already decided on a strategy of searching for stability, feared the potential for decline and would be happy to buy a home in a place that at least remained stable. Development is a sign that the physical and social environment will change, and some homebuyers feared that change was likely to be for the worse.

Additionally, younger homebuyers, who were currently raising children, also valued potential for stability. Sasha, 44, was looking to move out of a rental apartment into a house. She explained the qualities that she was looking for in a community:

> The diversity of the community, the taxes, the schools, its amenities as far as recreation, safety. Its representation, meaning its administration, are they handling the business of the community to make it safe. That's something I pay attention to now, considering I can see how a weak administration could weaken the community. I would want it to be stable and not have it not change often. I want it to be more stable.

Sasha is concerned not only about the current state of any community she might move into, but also about its future state. She is concerned both about safeguarding her financial investment (particularly about taxes) and about maintaining good quality of life. For Sasha and many of the homebuyers in this study, living in a racially diverse community was considered an important part of having a high quality of life. In part for the sake of her son, she wants to move to a community that has those ideal characteristics now and that appears to have potential for retaining those characteristics. She believes that having continuity in the local government is one possible sign that the desirable community characteristics will remain stable.

Signs of stability can sometimes result from familiarity and these can shape the use of the stability heuristic. A few of the homebuyers were most interested in buying somewhere familiar because it feels to them like a safe choice, even if the neighborhood dynamics are less than ideal. For instance, Anthony's first choice is to buy a home on the same block where his mother lives in his childhood home in Austin, a disadvantaged, predominately Black neighborhood on the West Side. While he works in shipping and receiving at a hospital, Anthony is currently living with his mother until he can save enough money to buy a house for his family. His fiancée and their children use a housing voucher to rent an apartment in Roseland where he cannot legally join them. He is extremely concerned about the safety of his children in Roseland because it is a high-crime neighborhood with which he is not familiar. By contrast, Anthony described his mother's neighborhood:

> I know all the neighbors and their children, and my kids are always with me in the summertime, so they know the neighborhood too, so—I don't have to worry about them too much. [...] I just feel safe and comfortable.

Interestingly, both Austin and Roseland consistently rank as high-crime community areas (Papachristos 2013). Because Anthony's number one goal is to reunite his family, moving to a lower-crime or more racially diverse area has not made it onto his list of priorities. While Roseland and Austin are similar in terms of crime statistics, he believes that he can keep his family safer in the area he knows well. Rosenblatt and DeLuca (2012) also found similar perceptions among Moving to Opportunity recipients who stayed in poor and violent neighborhoods because they felt confident in their ability to stay safe in these areas owing to their past experience. Stability is viewed through the lens of a particular racialized mental map of the city where some areas are more familiar and can be more easily trusted to remain stable than others.

Conclusion

As African American homebuyers attempt to change their neighborhood context, they must contend with a higher risk of neighborhood decline in the neighborhoods that comprise their choice set. As a result, they rely heavily on heuristics to predict future neighborhood trajectories. Homebuyers using the "avoiding decline" strategy tended to look for signs of the presence of voucher holders. Homebuyers use this indicator because they believe former public housing residents using housing vouchers will cause neighborhood decline. This idea is reinforced by the fact that voucher holders are not a clearly identifiable group. In his study of the housing voucher program in Los Angeles County, Rahim Kurwa (2015) found that race was used to identify, monitor, and stigmatize housing voucher holders.

In contrast, the Chicago metropolitan case demonstrates how stigmatization of voucher holders operates in areas where voucher holders are not racially distinct from other residents. In this case, homebuyers use stereotypes about voucher holders to identify members of this group, which serves to reinforce the stereotypes and heighten stigma. Ultimately, the emphasis on voucher holders obscures other factors related to racial change and neighborhood decline.

Understanding the combination of first-order neighborhood filtering, as well as the search heuristics employed subsequently, helps us to understand the process by which African Americans end up in racially segregated neighborhoods despite contrary stated desires. A set of first-order neighborhood filtering factors creates a situation in which homebuyers apply search heuristics to an already limited set of neighborhoods. Therefore, even geographically and socioeconomically mobile African Americans can find themselves stuck in a disadvantaged neighborhood context. In Chapter 6, I explain how these neighborhoods are disadvantaged and why the destination neighborhoods for the homebuyers are precarious in terms of the characteristics that are most important to homebuyers. In the next chapter, I turn my attention to how these homebuying processes were also shaped by public policy, specifically by homebuyer assistance programs.

Notes

1 Residential mobility is distinct from migration between regions, which Sharkey (2013) found was once higher than average for African Americans, but it has declined in recent decades.

2 Regents of the University of California v. Bakke, 438 U.S. 265 (1978).

References

Anderson, Matthew B., and Carolina Sternberg. 2012. "'Non-White' Gentrification in Chicago's Bronzeville and Pilsen: Racial Economy and the Intraurban Contingency of Urban Redevelopment." *Urban Affairs Review* 49(3): 435–467. https://doi.org/10.1177/1078087412465590.

Bader, Michael D. M., and Maria Krysan. 2015. "Community Attraction and Avoidance in Chicago: What's Race Got to Do with It?" *The Annals of the American Academy of Political and Social Science* 660(1): 261–281. https://doi.org/10.1177/0002716215577615.

Berrey, Ellen. 2015. *The Enigma of Diversity: The Language of Race and the Limits of Racial Justice*. Chicago: The University of Chicago Press.

Boyd, Michelle R. 2008. *Jim Crow Nostalgia: Reconstructing Race in Bronzeville*. Minneapolis: University of Minnesota Press.

Bruch, Elizabeth, and Fred Feinberg. 2017. "Decision-Making Processes in Social Contexts." *Annual Review of Sociology* 43(1): 207–227. https://doi.org/10.1146/annurev-soc-060116-053622.

Bruch, Elizabeth, Ross A. Hammond, and Peter M. Todd. 2015. "Coevolution of Decision-Making and Social Environments." In *Emerging Trends in the Social and Behavioral Sciences*, edited by R. A. Scott, S. M. Kosslyn, and M. Buchmann. New York: John Wiley & Sons.

Center on Budget and Policy Priorities. 2015. "Housing Choice Voucher Utilization Data Tables." National and State Housing Fact Sheets and Data. www.cbpp.org/research/housing/national-and-state-housing-fact-sheets-data#table1.

Covington, Kenya, Lance Freeman, and Michael Stoll. 2011. "The Suburbanization of Housing Choice Voucher Recipients." Metropolitan Opportunity series. Washington, D.C.: The Brookings Institution.

D'Rozario, Denver, and Jerome D. Williams. 2005. "Retail Redlining: Definition, Theory, Typology, and Measurement." *Journal of Macromarketing* 25(2): 175–86. https://doi.org/10.1177/0276146705280632.

Doering, Jan. 2020. *Us versus Them: Race, Crime, and Gentrification in Chicago Neighborhoods*. New York: Oxford University Press.

Freeman, Lance. 2011. *There Goes the 'Hood: Views of Gentrification from the Ground Up*. Philadelphia: Temple University Press.

Gigerenzer, Gerd, and Wolfgang Gaissmaier. 2011. "Heuristic Decision Making." *Annual Review of Psychology* 62(1): 451–482. https://doi.org/10.1146/annurev-psych-120709-145346.

Gigerenzer, Gerd, and Klaus Hug. 1992. "Domain-Specific Reasoning: Social Contracts, Cheating, and Perspective Change." *Cognition* 43(2): 127–171. https://doi.org/10.1016/0010-0277(92)90060-U.

Helling, Amy, and David S. Sawicki. 2003. "Race and Residential Accessibility to Shopping and Services." *Housing Policy Debate* 14(1–2): 69–101. https://doi.org/10.1080/10511482.2003.9521469.

Hwang, Jackelyn, and Robert J Sampson. 2014. "Divergent Pathways of Gentrification: Racial Inequality and the Social Order of Renewal in Chicago Neighborhoods." *American Sociological Review* 79(4): 726–751. https://doi.org/10.1177/0003122414535774.

Jun, Hee-Jung. 2016. "The Effect of Racial and Ethnic Composition on Neighborhood Economic Change: A Multilevel and Longitudinal Look." *Housing Studies* 31(1): 102–125. https://doi.org/10.1080/02673037.2015.1061108.

Kahneman, Daniel, and Amos Tversky. 1973. "On the Psychology of Prediction." *Psychological Review* 80(4): 237–251. https://doi.org/10.1037/h0034747.

Krysan, Maria, and Reynolds Farley. 2002. "The Residential Preferences of Blacks: Do They Explain Persistent Segregation?" *Social Forces* 80(3): 937–980. www.jstor.org/stable/3086462.

Kurwa, Rahim. 2015. "Deconcentration without Integration: Examining the Social Outcomes of Housing Choice Voucher Movement in Los Angeles County." *City & Community* 14(4): 364–391. https://doi.org/10.1111/cico.12134.

Marsh, Kris, and Kivan Polimis. 2014. "The Life Course Perspective in Explaining Racial Residential Segregation." In *Race, Space, and Exclusion: Segregation and Beyond in Metropolitan America*, edited by R.M. Adelman and C. Mele. New York: Routledge.

Massey, Douglas S., and Nancy A. Denton. 1993. *American Apartheid: Segregation and the Making of the Underclass*. Cambridge: Harvard University Press.

Mayorga-Gallo, Sarah. 2014. *Behind the White Picket Fence: Power and Privilege in a Multiethnic Neighborhood*. Chapel Hill: University of North Carolina Press.

Papachristos, Andrew V. 2013. "48 Years of Crime in Chicago: A Descriptive Analysis of Serious Crime Trends from 1965 to 2013." ISPS working paper ISPS13-023. New Haven: Institution for Social and Policy Studies, Yale University.

Pattillo, Mary. 2007. *Black on the Block: The Politics of Race and Class in the City*. Chicago: University of Chicago Press.

Perry, Evelyn M. 2016. *Live and Let Live: Diversity, Conflict, and Community in an Integrated Neighborhood*. Chapel Hill: The University of North Carolina Press.

Rosenblatt, Peter, and Stefanie DeLuca. 2012. "'We Don't Live Outside, We Live in Here': Neighborhood and Residential Mobility Decisions among Low-Income Families." *City & Community* 11(3): 254–284. https://doi.org/10.1111/j.1540-6040.2012.01413.x.

Sampson, Robert J. 2012. *Great American City: Chicago and the Enduring Neighborhood Effect*. Chicago: University of Chicago Press.

Sharkey, Patrick. 2013. *Stuck in Place: Urban Neighborhoods and the End of Progress Toward Racial Equality*. Chicago: University of Chicago Press.

Simon, Herbert A. 1987. "Satisficing." In *The New Palgrave: A Dictionary of Economics* 4: 243–245.

South, Scott J., and Glenn D. Deane. 1993. "Race and Residential Mobility: Individual Determinants and Structural Constraints." *Social Forces* 72(1): 147–167. https://doi.org/10.2307/2580163.

Swait, Joffre Dan. 1984. "Probabilistic Choice Set Generation in Transportation Demand Models." PhD thesis, Cambridge: Massachusetts Institute of Technology.

Swait, Joffre, and Moshe Ben-Akiva. 1987. "Incorporating Random Constraints in Discrete Models of Choice Set Generation." *Transportation Research Part B: Methodological* 21(2): 91–102. https://doi.org/10.1016/0191-2615(87)90009-9.

Swait, Joffre, and Tülin Erdem. 2007. "Brand Effects on Choice and Choice Set Formation under Uncertainty." *Marketing Science* 26(5): 679–697. www.jstor.org/stable/40057089.

Taylor, Monique M. 2002. *Harlem: Between Heaven and Hell*. Minneapolis: University of Minnesota Press.

Tversky, Amos, and Daniel Kahneman. 1973. "Availability: A Heuristic for Judging Frequency and Probability." *Cognitive Psychology* 5(2): 207–232. https://doi.org/10.1016/0010-0285(73)90033-9.

———. 1975. "Judgment under Uncertainty: Heuristics and Biases." In *Utility, Probability, and Human Decision Making*, edited by D. Wendt and C. Vlek. Boston: D. Reidel Publishing Company.

US Census Bureau. 2020. "Calculating Migration Expectancy Using ACS Data." US Census Bureau. www.census.gov/topics/population/migration/guidance/calculating-migration-expectancy.html.

———. 2014. "American Community Survey 2014 (5-Year Estimates)." Social Explorer Tables. US Census Bureau and Social Explorer.

Voorhees Center for Neighborhood and Community Improvement. 2014. "The Socioeconomic Change of Chicago's Community Areas (1970-2010)." Chicago: University of Illinois at Chicago.

Warikoo, Natasha K. 2016. *The Diversity Bargain: And Other Dilemmas of Race, Admissions, and Meritocracy at Elite Universities*. Chicago: University of Chicago Press.

5

FORECLOSURE MASH UNIT

The homebuyers were well aware of the potential for homeownership to go very wrong, in part because, at the time of this study, the fallout from the foreclosure crisis was still ongoing. The nonprofit agencies where I recruited the homebuyers were still attempting an emergency response to the crisis. Because these programs are understandably aimed at halting the damage from an ongoing crisis, other issues—including racial segregation—have been forced into the periphery. For instance, the South Suburban Housing Center (SSHC) was founded in 1975 to address housing discrimination and foster long-term diversity in the south suburbs of the Chicago metropolitan. The executive director of the SSHC, John R. Petruszak, explained the challenge facing his organization since the housing crisis:

> We are kind of like a MASH unit dealing with people who are bleeding to death right now. And we are trying to bring that under control. We are trying to do whatever we can to stop the bleeding. Once that's done and we can keep people in their homes and try to stabilize people where they are right now, then we can deal with expanding the housing markets [in the south suburbs].

Like many organizations involved in housing issues, SSHC has to focus on the immediate effects of the foreclosure crisis and do all that it can to assist the communities who were devastated by it. In Petruszak's reference to the eponymous TV show from the 1970s and early 1980s, the MASH unit approach to housing issues is due to the urgent and acute need for all the foreclosure-related services.

Furthermore, a great deal of funding from the government and other sources is tied to directly addressing this crisis. Consequently, less attention has been paid by these programs to the underlying issues of racial segregation. In this chapter, I demonstrate how current government assistance programs for homebuyers play a role in shaping neighborhood choice for African Americans, in some cases nudging homebuyers to remain in segregated neighborhoods. While attempting to stabilize neighborhoods that were hardest hit by the crisis is a noble goal, it is important not to lose sight of the dynamics of individual residential relocation decisions and the implications of those decisions for moving families.

Also, since homebuyers live in neighborhoods with renters, both renter housing policies and homeownership policies shape their experience of homeownership. Although most government housing dollars in the United States are spent on homeowners, the literature on housing policy has been more focused on policy as it relates to subsidizing renter housing costs. Here, I bring that research on government policy for renters into conversation with a discussion of policy for homeowners.

Dispersed Public Housing

As I discussed in Chapter 4, the working-class African American homebuyers in this study were heavily influenced by a theory of voucher-induced neighborhood decline. Many respondents blamed neighborhood decline (in different city neighborhoods and suburbs) on housing choice voucher (HCV) recipients and what they perceive as their inappropriate behavior. Jill's comments exemplify this divide:

> [I'm] always concerned about rentals, because people are transient. They're not setting roots. They're not invested in the community. Sometimes they don't bring progress. The homeowners, of course, are setting roots. They want to stay put. They are raising families. They are invested in the property. They are looking for good schools. They're making sure that there's adequate resources in the area.

It's worth noting that Jill thinks it is important to have specific kinds of neighbors because she believes she will have to rely on those neighbors to get "adequate resources." Something as fundamental as the necessary resources for a sustainable, safe community with good schools is not something that Jill can take for granted.

Similarly, Tabitha explained why she thinks changes in her area are related to more renters moving there:

> Because before, when you had a cluster of people who were maybe like-minded, for whatever reasons, I'm not casting aspersions, because I would say housing developments—I never use the term projects. I'm always respectful about people. It was more concentrated. Now what you've done is you've taken people out of those kinds of neighborhoods or living situations and

now they're interspersed throughout the community, and that has caused some problems.

As we can see, Tabitha adheres to the housing choice voucher theory of neighborhood decline that I found was a commonplace notion among the homebuyers. It is important to note that the dispersal she complains about is precisely the stated policy goal of the Chicago Housing Authority (CHA) and US Department of Housing and Urban Development (HUD). Tabitha is taking issue with the policy shift from concentrating subsidized rentals in specific, publicly owned housing developments to a dispersal of subsidized housing for renters. Despite a policy of dispersal, though, the bulk of those subsidized renters are still segregated in particular neighborhoods, which shapes how this policy affects Black homeowners and renters.

To understand how we arrived at a place where this conflict exists between working-class Black aspiring homebuyers and poor Black renters, we must take a look back at the history of rental assistance in the US. President Franklin D. Roosevelt's New Deal established the first national public housing for civilians. This program primarily built housing for working-class and middle-class Whites, and when housing was built for African Americans, it was segregated. This pattern continued for decades, and new public housing actually created racial segregation in areas that had previously been integrated. By the 1940s, more White people were able to find housing on the private market, and as a result, public housing projects that would have gone vacant were opened up to Black renters, but new public housing was mostly built in predominately Black areas. Civil rights activism around integrating public housing in the 1960s was necessarily focused on the placement of public housing in more integrated neighborhoods, because at that point few White families were applying for residence in these projects. In response, scattered-site public housing and voucher programs were intended to reverse the segregating effects of earlier public housing projects, but these efforts have been very limited compared with the large-scale of efforts to segregate public housing since its inception in the 1930s (Rothstein 2017).

Originally, public housing dispersal policy was intended to ameliorate the effects of previous racially discriminatory government action, but over time these programs have shifted their focus from race to class. Edward Goetz (2003) identifies and analyzes two main waves of public housing dispersal policy. The first wave occurred in the late 1960s to mid-1970s, and it was inspired by the fair housing movement aimed at ameliorating racial segregation. The Fair Housing Act of 1968, which was intended to address racial discrimination in housing, was enacted as a result of this movement. The actions taken by HUD to implement the Fair Housing Act have often been met with strong opposition. HUD attempted to disperse public housing under a regional fair share program in the early 1970s, but in the face of strong suburban opposition, scattered-site public housing remained very limited. By the early 1980s, scattered-site public housing made up only 9% of all assisted housing. The second wave of dispersal policy began in the 1990s under the Clinton administration. Concerns about concentrated poverty motivated this wave of interest in dispersal of public housing. In the early 1990s, Congress began to pay more attention to problems in public housing, including the fact that public housing projects contributed to concentrated poverty. The second wave of dispersal programs includes the Moving to Opportunity (MTO) demonstration program. This program was intended to test the benefits of deconcentrating poverty by dispersing subsidized renters in low-poverty areas. The experimental group in this program was actually required to move to low-poverty neighborhoods. Unlike the dispersal programs of the 1970s, the goal of MTO was class-based integration rather than racial integration.

In recent decisions on fair housing issues, the courts have also shifted their focus from remedying the racial segregation of public housing to remedying class-based segregation. In the *Gautreaux v. Chicago Housing Authority* housing discrimination case, the courts determined that the CHA and HUD had a role to play in remedying racial segregation.[1] In 1969, a federal judge in Chicago ordered CHA to build new public housing in non-minority neighborhoods. In 1976, the US Supreme Court upheld this decision and ordered HUD to create 7,100 Section 8 subsidies to be used in neighborhoods that were less than 30% African American (Popkin et al. 2000). The families who participated in the *Gautreaux* program were found to have long-term improvements in their neighborhood contexts even after subsequent moves (Keels et al. 2005). While CHA has continued to develop scattered-site programs, they have yet to live up to the promise of *Gautreaux* to ameliorate racial segregation.

The landmark *Gautreaux* ruling informs current HUD and CHA policy under Homeownership and Opportunity for People Everywhere (HOPE)VI and the Plan for Transformation. Enacted in 1992, HUD's HOPEVI plan called for: the demolition of racially and socioeconomically isolated, large public housing developments; and the creation of scattered-site, mixed-income housing. The CHA used HOPE VI funds to redevelop its largest and most infamous public housing developments including Cabrini–Green, Henry Horner, and Robert Taylor as part of the Plan for Transformation (Popkin et al. 2000). Despite the Plan for Transformation taking from *Gautreaux* the notion that dispersal of subsidized housing is beneficial, in practice, this plan does not directly address racial segregation.

Mary Pattillo (2008) describes how a major shift in the interpretation of *Gautreaux* occurred in 1981 through a consent decree allowing CHA to build in "revitalizing areas." These areas were defined as places with substantial minority populations that are undergoing enough redevelopment to suggest that they would integrate in the near future. The original *Gautreaux* decision clearly stated that CHA and HUD had racially discriminated against Black public housing tenants by deliberately placing them into racially segregated neighborhoods. The courts ordered CHA and HUD to move public housing residents to White neighborhoods in order to remedy this racial discrimination. While little progress had been made in racially desegregating public housing or neighborhoods in the Chicago metropolitan area, this 1981 consent decree allowed the CHA to change its focus from remedying racial segregation to a focus on socioeconomic integration when determining the location of subsidized housing.

The overall neighborhood context is important for how voucher recipients are received. A study in Baltimore County (Galster, Tatian, and Smith 1999) found that when Section 8 renters were located in wealthier, predominately White neighborhoods that had experienced previous increases in property values, these prices continued to rise.[2] On the other hand, in areas that they classified as vulnerable, which were moderately or low-valued areas that had already experienced a decline in housing prices in recent decades, a concentration of Section 8 households caused further decline. Furthermore, in more affluent areas, market-rate residents tended not to be aware of their subsidized neighbors, while in more vulnerable communities, residents were highly concerned about newcomers using rental vouchers and blamed them for problems. Other studies suggest that when subsidized housing is placed in highly stable, wealthier communities it can lead to better outcomes. For example, the Ethel Lawrence homes in Mount Laurel, New Jersey demonstrate how a well-designed public housing development can create stable class and racial integration (Massey et al. 2013). This mixed-income development was placed in a stable, middle-class, predominately White community with ample resources. Overall, the development has been considered a success, and it has seemingly not resulted in any negative effects in the surrounding areas.

Still, there is indeed some evidence that subsidized housing can have a negative effect on neighborhoods when it is overconcentrated. Property values are more likely to decline when the design and management of affordable units is poor and when subsidized housing is concentrated in already declining neighborhoods (Nguyen 2005). Large concentrations of voucher-holding households are associated with rising levels of crime in neighborhoods (Mast and Wilson 2013). With the mixed results of these studies, it is difficult to determine how close to the truth the theories of homebuyers are. Regardless, the fact that homebuyers act on these theories can make them a self-fulfilling prophecy akin to White flight, where White people act on their beliefs and projections about what others will do. The research suggests that dispersal of subsidized housing is important for the health of receiving neighborhoods.

In the case of Chicago's scattered-site public housing and voucher dispersal, subsidized housing has been disproportionately placed in African American communities that already face greater challenges. These communities are most likely to be harmed by a concentration of subsidized housing. While it is race-neutral on its face, Chicago's voucher program may be contributing to racial neighborhood inequality by maintaining racial segregation and concentrating subsidized housing in places that are least equipped to handle it successfully. Middle-income African American homebuyers are navigating the home-buying process in a landscape that has been affected by subsidized rental housing policy because subsidized housing falls disproportionately in predominately Black areas. The original promise of *Gautreaux* was to racially integrate public housing. By contrast, recent housing dispersal programs have exclusively pursued integration by socioeconomic class. By not making racial integration a priority when locating subsidized housing, recent efforts have left subsidized renters racially segregated. As a result, working-class African Americans feel that the project of integrating subsidized housing in terms of socioeconomic class has disproportionately affected them. If dispersed subsidized rental housing was truly dispersed—including in currently White and wealthy neighborhoods as well—the experience would be very different for working-class Black homebuyers.

Homebuyer Assistance Programs

While subsidies to renters are more commonly discussed than programs that assist homebuyers, many of the homebuyers in this study also benefited from housing subsidy programs (some of which are also funded by HUD). Policymakers must consider housing programs for renters and homebuyers together to understand their overall effect on neighborhood contexts and housing opportunity. Renters and homeowners are connected in that they share neighborhoods. And homebuyers consider who will be renting in their neighborhood when they select a place to buy a home.

In particular, the interviews in this study indicate that homebuyers are very concerned about subsidized rental policy and how it may affect neighborhoods in the future. Their concerns influence their purchasing choices, and as a result can affect housing markets. As I explained in Chapter 4, homebuyers are wary of renters as neighbors in general and associate homeowner status with middle-class respectability. At the same time, many of the aspiring homebuyers were very recently renters themselves. About 65% of the aspiring homebuyers were renting at the beginning of the study and others had rented previously. Because so many renters are aspiring homebuyers, the policies that inform the circumstances of renters will affect the ability of renters to become successful homeowners.

This link between renters and homebuyers was made clearer when I interviewed the neighbors of some of the homebuyers. These were people who lived within a few blocks of the homebuyers in this study, so they were not selected for attending a homebuyer education class, but desires for homeownership still came up in these interviews. For instance, Laila said she wanted to leave her current neighborhood in the City of Chicago for a suburb one day because "It's quiet" and "People own homes." She explained, "I'm going to buy me a home someday, so I want to buy me a home around people that I want to be around, so it's just something that I've always wanted for a long time." Her desires to have a piece of this particular American Dream—owning a home, in a quiet suburb—were quite similar to her neighbor whom I found through the homebuyer education class, who did move to a suburb. There is a paradox inherent in this ideal being held by renters—Laila is currently a renter and desires to eventually be a homebuyer surrounded by homebuyers. Making neighborhoods more exclusive, or accessible only to homeowners, is ultimately not a policy choice that will serve renters well, even when they aspire to be homebuyers, because, of course, not all aspiring homebuyers are able to buy a home (as this study demonstrates). Furthermore, homeownership is not a practical choice for everyone. Instead, we need to think about how housing policy for renters and homebuyers can work together to support these groups in being good neighbors for each other.

The homebuyers in this study all took part in homebuyer education classes, which are just one piece of the patchwork of assistance available to aspiring homebuyers. These homebuyer education classes were provided by two organizations with long histories in public policy and housing: the West Cook Homeownership Center (WCHC), and Neighborhood Housing Services (NHS). WCHC is a subsidiary of the Oak Park Regional Housing Center, which opened in 1972 to assist renters as part of Oak Park's program of intentional integration. The Oak Park Regional Housing Center was a major player in what Carole Goodwin (1979) calls the "Oak Park strategy," a collection of local policies aimed at preserving racial integration. Oak Park residents were deeply affected by their experience of watching Austin, the Chicago neighborhood that borders the suburb, go through a racial transition. As a result, racial integration became a part of the political conversation in Oak Park long before residents perceived racial change as an immediate threat. This, coupled with Oak Park's sense of its history as a community and civic-minded place, led community residents to develop a position in favor of preserving integration rather than halting it. Oak Park's attempts to control the process of racial change were always framed as efforts to maintain a stable integrated community (in other words, to avoid a demographic situation that would encourage White flight) rather than to keep Black people out. In practice, this process did involve limiting the number of Black renters and homebuyers who moved into the town and controlling which parts of the town they moved to at a time when Black people exhibited high demand for housing in the region. Oak Park leaders pursued their goal by developing a local fair housing ordinance with exempt locations in particular areas to "maintain racial balance," placing stringent regulations on the local real estate industry and carefully managing public relations for the town. Ultimately, this strategy has allowed Oak Park to become one of the few stable integrated communities in the region.

The Chicago branch of NHS was established in 1975 in an effort to revitalize struggling communities in the region and to assist homeowners in these areas. Its parent organization, NeighborWorks America, originally called the Neighborhood Reinvestment Corporation, is a national network of local Neighborhood Housing Services organizations. The first of these organizations began as a grassroots community group in Pittsburgh, Pennsylvania in 1971 with the goal of revitalizing declining inner-city neighborhoods. The organization expanded to other cities, and under the Carter administration, Congress created the Neighborhood

Reinvestment Corporation to support this work. In the 1990s, the organization launched the NeighborWorks Campaign for Homeownership, which focused on helping households achieve their homeownership goals. There are now 240 local NeighborWorks organizations operating in 50 states. The homebuyer education class offered by NHS is a prerequisite for a Homeownership Education Certificate, which some lenders require before issuing certain loans. Receiving this certificate can also make some buyers eligible for particular subsidies when purchasing a home. Both WCHC and NHS offer classes for prospective homebuyers with materials and training provided by NeighborWorks America, but only NHS is an official partner of NeighborWorks America.

It is worth noting how both of these organizations have changed their focus over time, in ways that brought their missions closer together around the issues of suburban revitalization and expanding homeownership. These changes reflect broader shifts in the focus of housing policy in the US. First, the Oak Park Regional Housing Center's initial purpose was to foster racial integration, while its subsidiary, WCHO, has moved on to a focus on revitalization and promoting homeownership. Meanwhile, NHS began as an organization aimed at revitalization, but of inner-city neighborhoods, and has eventually expanded to include revitalizing suburbs and promoting homeownership. Today, the organizations look somewhat similar in their focus on promoting homeownership and their inclusion of the suburbs as areas that they serve. These changes reflect a broader sense of growing need for assistance and revitalization in the suburbs, an interest in expanding homeownership, and a declining public focus on racial integration.

More recently, the foreclosure crisis shifted priorities for housing assistance programs, and both organizations were heavily involved with HUD-funded efforts to mitigate the effect of the crisis. Housing assistance programs that developed in the wake of the housing crisis, such as the Neighborhood Stabilization Program (NSP), focus on improving outcomes for neighborhoods rather than relocating individuals. While attempting to stabilize neighborhoods that were hardest hit by the crisis is a noble goal, it is important to not lose sight of the dynamics of individual residential relocation decisions and the implications of those decisions for moving families. Some of the homebuyers in this study received assistance through the NSP or were attempting to do so. NSP is a federal HUD program aimed at fostering development in neighborhoods that were hardest hit by the foreclosure crisis. It was first funded through the 2008 Housing and Economic Recovery Act, and received more funding in 2009 and 2010. HUD designed NSP to be geographically targeted at the most distressed areas. It is intended to provide an influx of funds that will stop an area from deteriorating owing to a high number of foreclosures. The purpose of the program is to avoid the negative externalities associated with high foreclosure rates, including higher crime rates and lowering home values for entire areas (Joice 2011).

It cannot be overstated that homebuyer assistance programs are helpful to and appreciated by middle-income African American aspiring homebuyers. The homebuyers in this study care deeply about achieving homeowner status and often privilege this goal above other concerns such as neighborhood context mobility. As I discussed in Chapter 2, Emma felt that becoming a homeowner greatly improved her sense of self and added to a sense of meaning in her life. Additionally, Emma attested to the invaluable role of both NHS and the Illinois Housing Development Authority (IHDA)—in short, she acknowledged that she "wouldn't have been able to do it at all." While she received a grant to cover her entire down payment through IHDA, that is not actually what she thought was the most important part of this assistance. Instead, Emma thought that "the biggest obstacle was the credit and they're the ones that put me in connection with the credit people. So, without that, I know I wouldn't have been able to do [it]." So, both the monetary assistance through the program and the housing counseling were greatly appreciated by homebuyers like Emma. The assistance put her on a better financial footing, giving her greater stability and enabling her to focus on creating the best home for her son. And it helped her to achieve an important life goal of improving her own idea of her status in society. At least sixteen of the sixty-eight homebuyers said in early interviews they were considering using a grant to aid their home purchase and of the twenty homebuyers whose complete moves were followed in this study, nine said they ultimately did receive a grant. Unlike some other forms of government assistance, receiving a homebuying grant does not come with negative stigma, and instead is associated with a firmer, more respectable place in society.

Other research has shown that the aspiring homebuyers in this study are not unusual in their strong desire to pursue the American Dream of homeownership. For instance, Camille Zubrinksy Charles (2006) found that in Los Angeles, 54% of Black non-homeowners said they would like to buy a house in the LA area compared with about half of White non-homeowners. For reasons that go beyond the economic, it is important to expand access to homeownership and to make that access more equitable along racial lines. Homebuyer assistance programs are expanding access, but they have not been constructed to take into account the existing racial dynamics in housing. It appears that some of the grant programs are not helping the homebuyers with the greatest need purchase in places that will give them the best returns on their investment, or place them in neighborhoods that meet their stated desires for diversity.

Vicki Been and Ingrid Gould Ellen (2009) suggest that while NSP is a well-intentioned program, if not implemented properly, it could exacerbate residential segregation by class. They point out that using neighborhood stabilization funds to place more subsidized housing in high-poverty neighborhoods will further concentrate poverty. It would essentially mean that the federal government would be repeating the same mistakes made previously with large public housing towers. Historically, HUD funded large, public housing tower complexes in many US cities and restricted them to very low-income tenants. These large public housing developments are widely understood to be at least partly responsible for the concentration of poverty, and they have also been found to contribute to racial segregation.

I believe NSP may also contribute to racial segregation. This program may encourage lower-income African Americans to make less integrative moves that will not improve their neighborhood context in the long run. In this case, the goal of stabilizing the predominately Black neighborhoods (which were hardest hit by the foreclosure crisis) may be at odds with the goal of improving residential outcomes for individual African American homebuyers. The City of Chicago has received funds from NSP to rehabilitate foreclosed homes and offer purchase assistance to buyers of rehabbed homes and homes in need of rehab. These homes are generally vacant, foreclosed, or short sale. A household of three making less than $54,750 can get $35,000 in purchase assistance; a household of three making less than $82,080 can get $25,000. NSP is focused on specific neighborhoods. In the NSP plan approved for Chicago in 2009, there were twenty-five eligible community areas. On average, these areas were 86% non-Hispanic Black. Other programs funded through NSP in the Chicago suburbs (including the West Cook Advantage program) operate similarly, and there are other similar down-payment assistance programs funded through different sources.

It was clear that NSP influenced homebuyers' choice sets by pushing homebuyers to consider neighborhoods that may not have been in their choice set originally. Cora, 32, works as a loan processor and is another aspiring homebuyer who was looking in the south suburbs. Cora mentioned that she was interested in South Holland and Lansing. When I asked when she had first learned about South Holland and Lansing, Cora replied, "When I spoke to a housing counselor." Prior to speaking with the housing counselor, Cora said:

> I was thinking about somewhere closer maybe to the city, maybe Evergreen Park or Oak Lawn, not so far out, but [those are] not too bad. I only started considering [South Holland and Lansing] because those are the areas in the program.

Similarly, Amanda, a 41-year-old custodian, was considering buying a home in Auburn Gresham or West Pullman in order "to get the additional funds." During our interview, Amanda pulled out a map she had of the areas covered by the NSP program and pointed to the ones she was interested in: "Yeah. These are the areas." She further explained that:

> Even though it says the different areas, you only have a certain amount of stretch in that area, so in Chatham [it includes] 79th to 83rd, from Cottage Grove to Queen Drive—too much crime in that area. I really don't want to live on the West Side up in these areas.

The program is designed to provide assistance in the areas with the greatest need of rehabilitation. Amanda would be interested in some blocks within the Chatham neighborhood, but not the blocks that are a part of the program because she believes they have high crime rates. Auburn Gresham was also an included neighborhood and, since she thought it was safer overall, Cora was willing to consider the parts of Auburn Gresham that were included in the program.

Similarly, William and Gloria were considering buying a home and rehabbing it with an NSP grant, but they decided against it because of the limited neighborhoods where this assistance was available:

> [The] neighborhood stabilization program picked Roseland and West Pullman, because they seem to have the biggest need for stabilizing, and I picked West Pullman near Roseland because of the fact that so many of the properties were being demolished, and it looked like it was [in] the bottom part of decline. We figured that this would probably be a community that would not drop greatly [below] what it is now. My wife wasn't in agreement with that, but that was something I was starting to look toward.

His wife, Gloria, explained that she had opposed this idea because she "didn't care for the area." They planned on moving with his elderly parents who currently lived in a suburb and Gloria felt that they could not "take them out of the mansion into the ghetto." The NSP program narrowed their choices too much, in her opinion because "Chicago's South Side is a briar patch of good places and places which you want to stay out of." With NSP focusing on the areas of most need of stabilization, it would push them towards the places she wanted to avoid.

Homebuyer assistance programs restrain homebuyers' choices in other ways that are not always obvious to homebuyers from the outset. Emma explained that a house she was interested in "was real-estate-owned" (meaning it was owned by a lender) "and the gas wasn't on, and IHDA will only approve funds if all the utilities are on, and real-estate-owned properties, they don't really do that." For Emma, in effect, not being able to purchase a real-estate-owned property made it difficult to access some neighborhoods she was interested in. The significance of the location of the homes that were available is heightened by the fact that the programs often make home purchases stickier. Emma also pointed out that she would probably stay in the home that she purchased until her young son "goes off to college, so another fourteen years, thirteen years." She added that "as part of the IDA thing, if I don't stay ten years, I've got to pay back the grant." Emma would not have necessarily been interested in moving sooner than that, but in her mind, the IHDA grant did make the move more long-term. Ultimately, that means that this homebuying decision will shape where her son spends most of his school-age years, influencing the resources that are available to them during this important time.

Homebuyers in this study did not generally consider the NSP-targeted areas very desirable, but they were sometimes swayed to consider them because of the purchase assistance offered by NSP. Because Black households have lower levels of wealth, they are more likely to find it difficult to save enough for a down payment. NSP may be inadvertently creating a new form of racial steering by offering the type of assistance most needed by Black households in predominately Black areas. While expanding access to ownership is an admirable goal, it is insufficient if homebuyers continue to buy in segregated neighborhoods or neighborhoods with a high likelihood of becoming resegregated. Disparities in housing value appreciation created by racial segregation continue to harm African Americans' ability to build wealth (Shapiro 2006). Therefore, programs like NSP will contribute to these problems unless they take into account racial dynamics in housing.

Conclusion

In many ways, the down-payment programs that are currently operating to address the consequences of the foreclosure crisis are an emergency response. Because these programs are understandably aimed at halting the damage from an ongoing crisis, other issues—including racial segregation—have been forced into the periphery. SSHC is one example of an organization that has tried to design its foreclosure crisis-related programs to be as oriented towards furthering fair housing as possible. As part of its fair housing enforcement efforts, SSHC comprised part of an investigation into the maintenance of real-estate-owned properties (that is, homes owned by lenders as a result of foreclosure). This investigation found that banks were systematically neglecting the maintenance of houses that they owned (as a result of foreclosures) in majority minority suburban neighborhoods. SSHC helped to file a fair housing complaint on the basis of this investigation and received funds from a settlement with Wells Fargo. Along with other neighborhood improvement efforts, SSHC are using these funds to give down-payment assistance grants to homebuyers purchasing in effected neighborhoods.

Derek T. Adkisson, SSHC's Director of Finance and Operations—who designed the down-payment assistance program—explained how the program aligns with their overall fair housing goals (personal interview, July 25, 2016). Most importantly, unlike some of the other down-payment assistance programs, the SSHC program does not have an income cap. By not capping the program, they hope to provide an incentive for higher-income buyers to purchase in these more distressed areas, and, by proxy, this may encourage more racially integrative moves. One potential issue with this approach is that higher-income buyers may be less motivated by the down-payment assistance. A second potential problem is that the higher-income buyers with fewer assets may be more motivated to pursue down-payment assistance, and this group is likely to be disproportionately African American. Regardless, making the down-payment assistance in distressed areas available to higher-income buyers is an improvement over other similar down-payment assistance programs in terms of encouraging integrative moves. This program suggests possibilities for combining efforts to ameliorate damage from the foreclosure crisis with initiatives that encourage residential integration.

Notes

1 Gautreaux v. Chicago Housing Authority, 296 F. Supp. 907 (N.D. Ill. 1969).
2 This study of Baltimore County did not find that the racial demographics of the neighborhood changed the effect of subsidized housing on home values. But the researchers found it difficult to separate the effects of racial demographics because there was not enough variation in the socioeconomic status of the predominately minority neighborhoods. All of the racially mixed and predominately Black neighborhoods in this study fell into the vulnerable category, which was more strongly affected by increases in subsidized housing.

References

Been, Vicki, and Ingrid Gould Ellen. 2009. "In the Wake of the Foreclosure Crisis: Targeting Neighborhood Stabilization Funds." New York: Furman Center for Real Estate and Urban Policy, New York University.

Charles, Camille Zubrinksy. 2006. *Won't You Be My Neighbor?: Race, Class, and Residence in Los Angeles*. New York: Russell Sage Foundation.

Galster, George C., Peter Tatian, and Robin Smith. 1999. "The Impact of Neighbors Who Use Section 8 Certificates on Property Values." *Housing Policy Debate* 10(4): 879–917. https://doi.org/10.1080/10511482.1999.9521354.

Goetz, Edward G. 2003. "Housing Dispersal Programs." *Journal of Planning Literature* 18(1): 3–16. https://doi.org/10.1177/0885412203251339.

Goodwin, Carole. 1979. *The Oak Park Strategy: Community Control of Racial Change*. Chicago: University of Chicago Press.

Joice, Paul A. 2011. "Neighborhood Stabilization Program." *Cityscape* 13(1): 135–141. https://dx.doi.org/10.2139/ssrn.1808957.

Keels, Micere, Greg J. Duncan, Stefanie DeLuca, Ruby Mendenhall, and James Rosenbaum. 2005. "Fifteen Years Later: Can Residential Mobility Programs Provide a Long-Term Escape from Neighborhood Segregation, Crime, and Poverty." *Demography* 42(1): 51–73. https://doi.org/10.1353/dem.2005.0005.

Massey, Douglas S., Len Albright, Rebecca Casciano, Elizabeth Derickson, and David N. Kinsey. 2013. *Climbing Mount Laurel: The Struggle for Affordable Housing and Social Mobility in an American Suburb*. Princeton: Princeton University Press.

Mast, Brent D., and Ronald E. Wilson. 2013. "Housing Choice Vouchers and Crime in Charlotte, NC." *Housing Policy Debate* 23(3): 559–596. https://doi.org/10.1080/10511482.2013.794853.

Nguyen, Mai Thi. 2005. "Does Affordable Housing Detrimentally Affect Property Values? A Review of the Literature." *Journal of Planning Literature* 20(1): 15–26. https://doi.org/10.1177/0885412205277069.

Pattillo, Mary. 2008. *Black on the Block: The Politics of Race and Class in the City*. Chicago: University of Chicago Press.

Popkin, Susan J., Larry F. Buron, Diane K. Levy, and Mary K. Cunningham. 2000. "The Gautreaux Legacy: What Might Mixed-Income and Dispersal Strategies Mean for the Poorest Public Housing Tenants?" *Housing Policy Debate* 11(4): 911–942.
Rothstein, Richard. 2017. *The Color of Law: A Forgotten History of How Our Government Segregated America*. New York: Liveright Publishing Corporation.
Shapiro, Thomas M. 2006. "Race, Homeownership and Wealth." *Washington University Journal of Law & Policy* 20: 53–74.

6

PRECARIOUS DESTINATIONS

Kimberly, a 38-year-old social worker living in the predominately Black Woodlawn neighborhood on Chicago's South Side, had just purchased a home in South Holland, in part because she wants to live in a more racially diverse community. She said she chose to move from the predominately Black South Side neighborhood of West Woodlawn to a suburb in order to raise her son in a more diverse community:

> *Kimberly*: I prefer a mixed environment. I don't want to live in an all-African American environment. I definitely don't want to live in an all-Caucasian environment, but somewhere mixed. Because I am raising my thirteen-year-old son, cultural values and cultural diversity are important to me.
>
> *Interviewer*: In terms of economic status [do], you want a neighborhood that's mixed?
>
> *Kimberly*: No. I must live in a middle-class environment, total opposite of where I come from. However, the majority of—[Woodlawn]—that environment is impoverished. However, you do have people like myself who are educated, who do work every day, who are considered middle-class. Those people do exist in that population despite of what the news says. But I am looking more so for a middle-class environment.

Kimberly believes that the wider world paints people who live in predominately Black neighborhoods with one broad brush. She hopes that moving to a more racially diverse neighborhood will help her and her son escape the burden of these racist stereotypes.

Because Kimberly wants to live in a more racially diverse area, it is interesting that she chose a home in South Holland, which appears to be experiencing White flight. She also considered the Lincoln Park neighborhood and the suburbs of Willowbrook and Aurora, which all have smaller proportions of Black residents. Kimberly's personal connections played a large part in where she ultimately moved—she ended up buying a home in South Holland through a private sale from friends she knows from church. I asked, "So for South Holland, how would you say that does or does not sort of match up with the things that you were looking for in a community?" She replied:

> It matches up. It definitely matches up (laughs). I don't know if this is politically correct, but I'm in the good part of South Holland because as all neighborhoods, once you cross lines or territories or boundaries, the community can better or worsen. Well, I am in a better part of South Holland.

I asked Kimberly about the racial makeup of her new neighborhood, and she noted, "Out of one hundred percent, I can say maybe sixty percent African American, forty percent Caucasian, ten percent Hispanic." According to the 2014 American Community Survey, the census block group where she had bought a house was about 14% White, 86% Black, and 1% Hispanic. The area in Woodlawn where she is moving from is nearly 100% Black. South Holland is more diverse, but less White than Kimberly thinks it is. It is possible that Kimberly based her perceptions on conversations with family and friends about neighborhoods and on past visits to the area, and both of these sources and perspectives lag behind the process of racial change, which has been fairly quick in South Holland. The suburb overall went from 0.5% Black in 1980 to 74% in 2010. Like Kimberly, most of the homebuyers were satisfied with the places that they moved, even several months after moving. They generally felt that they had been successful in achieving their housing goals.

But, the places that they moved to do not look like places that are likely to retain these characteristics for the long term. They were often the kinds of places that are at risk of shifting from the racially integrated middle-class neighborhoods they wanted, or not changing fast enough into the gentrifying neighborhoods they desired. In the end, despite interest in racially diverse neighborhoods with greater amenities, homebuyers often end up in fairly similar places to the neighborhoods they were leaving behind. Twenty of the homebuyers provided final addresses in follow-up interviews. Fifteen aspiring homebuyers were still working on building credit, saving, or house hunting at the time of our last contact, while seven had stopped searching. Table 6.1 shows characteristics of the origin and destination neighborhoods for the homebuyers who provided final addresses. On average, the neighborhoods they moved to had a slightly smaller percentage of African American residents (11% less) and were slightly higher-income ($8,891.60 higher), but many homebuyers remained in similar areas to where they began. These findings are in line with findings that low-income and minority homebuyers buy in similar places to where they rent. In other words, homeownership does not tend to improve neighborhood quality. Those homebuyers who saw the largest changes in racial demographics and biggest increases in median household income between their origin and destination neighborhoods were often moving to suburbs that appear to be undergoing racial transitions. It is unclear how stable the demographics of these neighborhoods will be in the future.

Of course, for homebuyers interested in neighborhoods that they predict will improve, it may not be surprising that their destination neighborhoods do not look demographically different at the time of their move. Homebuyers who were interested primarily in improvement were often highly optimistic in their projections for gentrification in neighborhoods where they want to buy homes. On the other hand, due to the first-order filtering process, the options that they were considering rarely had a high potential for gentrification.

Gentrification Aspirations and Realities

Most of the homebuyers interested in improvement in this study were looking in predominately Black neighborhoods, despite limited past instances of gentrification in Black neighborhoods. Matthew Anderson and Carolina Sternberg claim that persistent negative attitudes toward predominately Black neighborhoods (even those with substantial middle-class populations) makes them much more resistant to White gentrification than Hispanic neighborhoods in Chicago (Anderson and Sternberg 2013). The Voorhees Center for Neighborhood and Community Improvement at UIC (2014) developed an index to show socioeconomic change in neighborhoods from 1970 to 2010, and they find that much more of Chicago has declined than has experienced gentrification. The areas that homebuyers are hoping will experience gentrification are not close to the areas that have gentrified during this period and are not similar to them in terms of racial demographics.

For the most part, the homebuyers' ideas about gentrification were not derived from their own experiences, because they had usually not lived in gentrifying neighborhoods previously. Instead, their ideas about gentrification came mainly from encounters with gentrification talk, with friends and family, in the media and with real estate agents. Attitudes towards gentrification are likely to differ between those who have experienced it firsthand and those who have mostly heard about gentrification in the media or from realtors. It seems likely that if Chicago's patterns of gentrification were as extensive and fast-paced as what New York City has seen in recent decades, the homebuyers in this study would have more varied and complex opinions on gentrification, similar to those Lance Freeman (2011) found among Black residents of Harlem.

For the homebuyers I talked to, gentrification was seen as a route to economic success through homeownership. Elizabeth was a 52-year-old college graduate

TABLE 6.1 Demographics of the Zip Codes at Homebuyers' Origin Addresses and the Zip Codes Where They Bought Homes, Using Data from the 2015 American Community Survey and the 2010 Census

Homebuyer	*Origin zip code*	*% Non-Hispanic Black at origin zip code 2010*	*Median house value for all owner-occupied housing units 2015*	*Median household income (in 2015 inflation-adjusted dollars) 2015*	*Destination zip code*	*% Non-Hispanic Black 2010 at destination zip code*	*Median house value for all owner-occupied housing units 2015 at destination zip code*	*Median household income (in 2015 inflation-adjusted dollars) 2015 at destination zip code*	*Change in % non-Hispanic Black*	*Change in median income*
Amira	60618	2.8%	$320,600	$57,500	60615	61.3%	$231,700	$41,108	58.5%	-$ 16,392.00
Cindy	60637	78.1%	$171,800	$26,845	60637	78.1%	$171,800	$26,845	0.0%	$ -
Elizabeth	60632	1.6%	$162,400	$38,438	60609	28.2%	$160,800	$32,284	26.6%	-$ 6,154.00
Alicia	60466	58.7%	$80,900	$44,174	60429	81.6%	$112,500	$51,141	22.9%	$ 6,967.00
Andrew	60438	30.7%	$129,900	$48,820	60466	58.7%	$80,900	$44,174	28.0%	-$ 4,646.00
Bridget	60620	97.7%	$132,300	$32,168	60620	97.7%	$132,300	$32,168	0.0%	$ -
Emma	60628	94.2%	$119,200	$36,242	60628	94.2%	$119,200	$36,242	0.0%	$ -
Hannah	60620	97.7%	$132,300	$32,168	60628	94.2%	$119,200	$36,242	-3.5%	$ 4,074.00
Jennifer	60628	94.2%	$119,200	$36,242	60634	1.0%	$230,700	$56,382	-93.2%	$ 20,140.00
Jill	60620	97.7%	$132,300	$32,168	60803	16.5%	$158,700	$52,100	-81.2%	$ 19,932.00
Kaya	60619	96.8%	$141,400	$32,239	60411	48.6%	$102,900	$41,188	-48.2%	$ 8,949.00
Kimberly	60637	78.1%	$171,800	$26,845	60473	73.6%	$151,700	$66,096	-4.5%	$ 39,251.00
Michelle	60104	74.7%	$118,800	$49,467	60107	4.2%	$173,100	$75,129	-70.5%	$ 25,662.00
Patricia	60629	22.4%	$141,000	$40,712	60430	34.3%	$166,000	$69,028	11.9%	$ 28,316.00

Ruth	60643	74.0%	$174,400	$52,100	60461	69.5%	$241,300	$95,192	-4.5%	$ 43,092.00
Tabitha	60302	22.1%	$380,600	$76,784	60302	22.1%	$380,600	$76,784	0.0%	$ -
Alice	60302	22.1%	$380,600	$76,784	91945	13.0%	$316,600	$55,801	-9.1%	-$ 20,983.00
Libby	60478	85.1%	$130,200	$54,608	60430	34.3%	$166,000	$69,028	-50.8%	$ 14,420.00
Keshia	60628	94.2%	$119,200	$36,242	60628	94.2%	$119,200	$36,242	0.0%	$ -
Sarah	60426	77.1%	$76,600	$23,362	60409	70.0%	$100,200	$38,566	-7.1%	$ 15,204.00
Average		65.0%	$166,775	$42,695		53.8%	$171,770	$51,587	-11.2%	$ 8,891.60

earning her primary income driving for a rideshare taxi service. Speaking of the house she hoped to buy, Elizabeth said:

> It has to be in a neighborhood that is up and coming. I want to invest. I want something that I'm going to be paying into to appreciate and I want it to be able to have a nice increase in equity.

Elizabeth did end up buying a home in New City. While rising home values were one of Elizabeth's stated reasons for choosing to buy in New City, that does not appear to be the trajectory for her area in recent years. Adjusting for inflation to 2017 values, the median home value for the census block group where she bought a home was $182,792 in 2009 and down to $168,400 in 2017 (see Figure 6.1).

While desire for accumulation of savings is the most obvious reason that Black homebuyers might desire gentrification, it was not the only reason. One homebuyer named Lucy, 57, had previously moved to a neighborhood that she believed was "up and coming," but years later she was disappointed with the lack of change it actually experienced. She moved to South Shore hoping it would become a more racially diverse environment, which she associates with middle-class amenities. She later wanted to leave because the change was not coming quickly enough:

> It's changing slowly, but it's noticeable. I would say right now it's about maybe ninety-five percent Black with more Whites moving in. Some of those buildings that are being turned into condos, and I do notice in the mornings when I'm leaving for work, I see more Whites walking their dogs

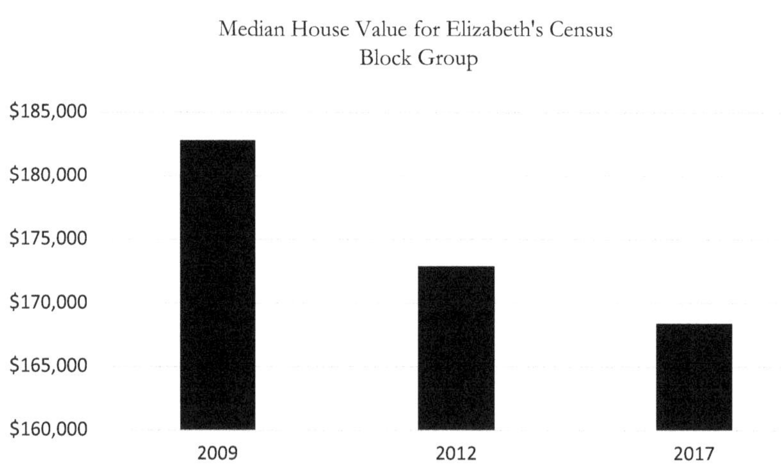

FIGURE 6.1 Median House Value for All Owner-Occupied Housing Units Using Data from the American Community Survey for the Census Block Group Where Elizabeth Bought a Home. Dollars are Adjusted for Inflation to Match Value in 2017

> and stuff than I did when I first moved in ten years ago. So, it's slowly changing, but I don't want to be around, I just—It's so slow that it's not worth the wait.

Lucy says of the area she wants to move to, that: "It would be more mixed. In certain areas over there depends on how far west you go. You would have Blacks, Whites, and Hispanics." Lucy had thought at one time that South Shore would undergo socioeconomic and racial change. She even thinks that she has seen some slow signs of that change, but she is still disappointed by the degree to which things have stayed the same. The danger inherent in using the improvement heuristic is the risk that things will remain the same.

And for those who bought in places that they thought would gentrify, the results can be devastating. In her memoir, reporter Natalie Moore described how she found herself $100,000 underwater for her mortgage on a condo in Bronzeville, meaning that she owed that much more on the house than it was worth (Moore 2016). Bronzeville has experienced some limited middle-class Black gentrification, but despite extensive efforts to promote residential and retail investments in the area, it has remained relatively disadvantaged, and a poor investment.

Much like Natalie Moore, Tiffany, who as I mentioned in Chapter 1 had seen her parents lose money in a suburb that experienced White flight, was particularly interested in purchasing a home in Bronzeville. Tiffany had some ambivalent feelings about gentrification but was generally excited about the prospect: "Well, on one hand, the fact that some of us that cannot afford the expensive homes, it's almost like we're getting priced out and we have to move into a neighborhood that may not be as safe." But, she also expressed her general support for gentrification:

> [It is] mostly positive, because you know, I'd love to live in an up-and-coming area or area that has huge improvements such as new homes being built. They're beautiful. I love to see diversity in the area, you know? It's not just African Americans in the world. So, I love to see people walking about, enjoying life, walking their dog, being friendly.

Tiffany was not the only homebuyer to mention people "walking their dogs" as an important and positive aspect of gentrification. There seemed to be a general hope that gentrification might improve the neighborliness of the community, not just bringing racial diversity, but also allowing for different kinds of people to come into contact with one another.

Stability Aspirations and Realities

Homebuyers who were most interested in stability were generally buying in more diverse neighborhoods. This choice makes sense because they were buying in places that already have the characteristics that they want in a neighborhood, with the hope that they will retain those characteristics. Unfortunately, because the first-order filtering process ruled out some of the most stable neighborhoods in terms of the demographic characteristics that mattered to homebuyers, these homebuyers were often looking in White-flight areas. These neighborhoods and towns still have some White residents, but have shown large increases in the proportion of Black residents in recent years. Furthermore, homebuyers most interested in stability also tended to be older homebuyers with children who were most interested in suburbs, and many suburbs to the south and west of Chicago are current sites of White flight. To illustrate this change, Table 6.2 shows African American population growth for the suburbs where homebuyers in this study bought homes. These homebuyers were chasing a particularly popular version of the American Dream of homeownership—the suburban dream. As pointed out by Orly Clergé (2019), who also studied Black suburbs, buying a suburban home can feel like the ultimate achievement of the dream, but the ability to fully live out the dream in that space continues to be contested.

The homebuyers who bought in these racially transitioning suburbs usually felt successful in their moves. Because they saw their search for home through the lens of the search heuristics that they used during the active part of their search, they believed that they had actively searched for and found stable or

TABLE 6.2 Demographic Data and Change Over Time in Suburbs Where Homebuyers Bought Homes. Data is from the 2000 and 2010 Census

Homebuyer	*Destination suburbs*	*Percent Non-Hispanic Black 2000*	*Percent Non-Hispanic Black 2010*	*Percent change in non-Hispanic Black population 2000–2010*
Jill	Alsip, IL	10%	17.90%	74%
Michelle	Berkeley, IL	28%	30.91%	11%
Marlon	Calumet City, IL	53%	69.89%	26%
Alicia	Hazel Crest, IL	76%	84.65%	6%
Patricia	Homewood, IL	17%	33.74%	92%
Libby	Homewood, IL	17%	33.74%	92%
Kaya	Lynwood, IL	45%	65.35%	76%
Tabitha	Oak Park, IL	22%	21.25%	-6%
Ruth	Olympia Fields, IL	52%	68.89%	40%
Andrew	Park Forest, IL	39%	59.05%	42%
Kimberly	South Holland, IL	51%	73.82%	45%
	Average	37%	51%	45%

improving neighborhoods in terms of their ideal demographic characteristics. For instance, Kaya wanted to move to a more racially diverse area than her current predominately Black city neighborhood, but she ended up in a racially transitioning suburb. I asked her to describe one suburb that she said would be an ideal area to move to: "Well, it's not too far. I've always traveled there a lot, and it's a mixed community." Kaya wanted three things in her new community—she wants it to be some place familiar, a place that isn't too far away from the area of the city when she lived before, and she wanted greater racial diversity. Ultimately, she moved to Lynwood, Illinois, which would appear to meet all of these criteria. It's a south suburb about a thirty-minute drive from where she previously lived in the city. The zip code she moved to is 48.6% Black, while the town overall is 65.4% Black. The area is less Black than the zip code she moved from, which was 96.8% Black, but from 2000 to 2010 Lynwood had 76% Black population growth. It appears to be an area at risk for a racial transition that would make it less likely to meet Kaya's criteria in the future. Ultimately, moving somewhere that felt familiar and more central based on her racialized map of the city prevented her from moving to a place with stable racial demographics.

Because first-order filtering often eliminated more potentially racially stable areas, homebuyers who were actively using the stability heuristics often still buy homes in racially transitioning neighborhoods. For these reasons, homebuyers believe themselves to be actively searching for and often finding homes in neighborhoods with their ideal characteristics, despite the fact that demographic statistics may paint a different picture of these neighborhoods. Homebuyers who were interested in stability used this heuristic because they wanted to live in neighborhoods with particular characteristics at the moment. They had pressing present needs for a quality neighborhood due to their particular family situation and life stage. So, they bought homes in places that have those characteristics at the moment, hoping that they would not change. Unfortunately, this combination of first-order filtering and search heuristics applied to the remaining set of potential areas, which then left homebuyers looking in neighborhoods that may suffer from subsequent decline and suppressed housing markets.

On average, the suburbs that homebuyers moved to were 51% African American in 2010 and had a 45% growth in their African American population from 2000 to 2010. The city zip codes where homebuyers moved had an average percentage of African American or Black residents of 64%. We know that the consequence of Black families buying in White-flight neighborhoods is a loss of wealth because of how these neighborhoods are disadvantaged in a racialized housing market. Even if these communities stabilize at the current percentage of Black residents, these areas are already at risk for lower home value appreciation (Shapiro 2004). Junia Howell and Elizabeth Korver-Glenn (2020) found that home appraisers continue to use racialized assumptions about neighborhoods to determine home values, causing neighborhood racial composition to be a stronger determinate of appraised home values in 2015 than in 1980.

One could imagine that declining home values may not be a serious concern to some homebuyers, especially if they are purchasing in places where prices are already relatively low. A homebuyer could rationally choose a discount on their current housing costs with the trade-off that their home will not be a valuable investment later. But this was not how the homebuyers discussed their choice of homes. Many were excited about what their investment would mean for future generations in their families. After purchasing her home, Libby speculated:

> I imagine we probably will have a lot of grandkids, just because we have a lot of kids. So, them coming to enjoy it would be great. I would love to like keep it a family house. You know, whenever something happens to us, then it's passed down to the kids, or if they want to give it to their kids or whatever.

The dream of establishing a "family house" that will provide shelter, community, and financial stability for generations to come is only possible when purchasing in a neighborhood that is stable or improving. Unfortunately, racially disparate housing market outcomes make this goal extremely difficult for African Americans to attain. This long-term decline in housing values is not due to lack of concern for future outcomes or lack of effort.

Satisfaction with Location of New Home

Despite the potential precarity of the places where homebuyers were purchasing homes, most felt happy with their purchases shortly after the move. Homebuyers were either optimistic about improvement in their neighborhoods or confident that their neighborhoods would remain stable. If you simply used a survey to ask the homebuyers who purchased a home if their homebuying process has been successful and if they ended up with a home in the kind of area that they wanted, the vast majority would say yes. The deeper question is whether these purchases will help them secure a foothold in the middle class and whether these places will continue to have the characteristics that they value for years to come.

Leaving the Region

I first spoke with Tiffany about her desire to buy a home in 2015, and in the summer of 2018 she still had not purchased a home. Over the course of those years, she vacillated over whether to buy in her neighborhood or leave the region altogether. While she was optimistic about improvements in her neighborhood, she also had concerns about its current problems. She still felt that the neighborhood was not safe enough for her 15-year-old son to be out and about on his own. She had long been interested in purchasing the condo that she was renting from the current owner, but the condo building had financial issues that made it more difficult to get a mortgage loan (the percentage of renters was too high and the association did not have enough funds in reserve). So while she waited, she also thought about moving to Texas or somewhere else on the West Coast or in the South. Tiffany likes Texas for the climate, the lower cost of living, and lower taxes. To escape what they saw as the problems of Chicago, a few homebuyers discussed the possibility of leaving the region for Sun Belt states. No one can really predict the future of real estate and say whether the better choice for Tiffany is Bronzeville or Texas, but the trajectories of Bronzeville and similar neighborhoods suggest that her skittishness about purchasing there is warranted.

Another aspiring homebuyer, Alice, did successfully leave the region for San Diego. We spoke on the phone after she relocated to Southern California. Alice moved there because:

> I used to work for an airline years ago […] and checked out Florida, Arizona, Hawaii, and California. […] San Diego has the most temperate weather in the United States. Average is 73 year-round, and that appealed to me, and the fact that there's a lot of military opportunities for love and for dating. [laughs] […] And job opportunities with the federal government. Got a lot of military guys here, and we've got a lot of military work here.

She also appreciates that "San Diego is very integrated. […] You see everybody in every neighborhood. So that's pretty cool, Asian, Hispanic, Black, White." Her only disappointment after the move was that the pizza was "not like Chicago." These Sun Belt areas appeal to some homebuyers' desire for a change from the Chicago metropolitan area for a variety of reasons; greater racial integration is not the only reason, but it is a factor.

Deciding Not to Buy

Homebuyers had difficulty identifying stable, racially diverse neighborhoods because of the existing racial demographics in the Chicago metropolitan region and the buyers' tendency to focus on the portions of the metropolitan region that have the largest existing Black population. One aspiring homebuyer, Samantha, was so apprehensive about her ability to identify a stable neighborhood that met her other requirements that she decided against pursuing homeownership. Samantha decided to continue renting an apartment rather than buy because she did not trust the stability of the housing market where her family already lives, Forest Park, a racially diverse suburb to the west of Chicago. Because I recruited participants from homebuyer counseling events, I had very few respondents who, like Samantha, had made a deliberate decision to rent. She compared Forest Park with the farther-out suburb of Naperville, which she thought was a safer place to buy:

> Because I think Naperville is a growing neighborhood. Right now, the rent is low, like you can find quality stuff there, but I don't think that it's diverse. I think Naperville is low now and will increase, but for Forest Park, the costs are higher, and I feel like it can't get that much higher.

When Samantha says that Naperville "is not diverse," the difference between the two suburbs she alludes to is that Forest Park has a growing Black population that reached 32% in 2010, whereas Naperville was less than 5% Black in 2010 (US Census Bureau 2010). Because Samantha wants to live in a diverse neighborhood with a significant Black population, she is not interested in moving to Naperville despite its stronger housing market. In this case, the challenge of finding stability made homeownership unappealing.

Still Struggling

In contrast to the homebuyers who were able to purchase a home, many were disappointed and frustrated to still be struggling with the process years later. As I called and emailed the homebuyers to ask how their homebuying process had progressed, I sometimes felt like a nag. My calls would be answered wearily, as homebuyers did not like the reminder of how long the process had taken them. At the time, as a PhD candidate who was still working on my dissertation, I could relate to not wanting to answer questions about progress towards a goal! Some aspiring homebuyers, who had happily chatted away in earlier calls, refused later interviews because it was just too disappointing to talk about. Meanwhile, others enjoyed the ongoing opportunity to blow off steam about their frustrations with the process. I learned to avoid mentioning how long it had been since the first time we had talked. As I discussed in Chapter 3, obstacles preventing homebuyers from achieving their dream included credit problems, lack of savings, and precarious financial circumstances.

While the foreclosure crisis lowered prices and made a lot of homes available to new buyers, it created some challenges as well. First, the process of buying a foreclosed home is often different from a more traditional home sale. It is an understatement to say that it can be difficult for individuals to navigate. As a result, these kinds of sales are often dominated by investors. For instance, Michelle described her experience looking for a home:

> A lot of the foreclosed properties, they want cash. I don't have cash, so even though I may be able to get approved for certain amounts, these properties

> that are in foreclosure, they want fast money. [...] They're mostly looking for people who are just flipping properties.

This meant that a large portion of the homes in the neighborhood she was most interested in were simply not available to her. In addition, these foreclosed homes have sometimes been vacant. They may need more repairs. These can create difficult situations for buyers with little experience of homeownership and limited resources. It's much more difficult to get a loan to cover the costs of home improvements than it is to get a home mortgage.

Furthermore, empty foreclosed homes drag down the property values around them and harm the quality of life in neighborhoods. They create risky situations which are evident to perspective buyers and may discourage them from buying at all. Sarah was frustrated with all of the foreclosed properties in her neighborhood:

> I feel if you kept the people in the house until you sell the house, the neighborhood would look more upcoming than down fall, and to me it seems like why would you kick them out and make the house go down for nothing? And make the neighborhood go down for nothing? Because when the house go down, then that's when the neighborhood go down.

During the time of this research, the government-funded housing assistance programs that I discussed in Chapter 5 were directed at solving this very problem—the neighborhood blight and housing market distress caused by foreclosed properties. Despite this issue being a persistent concern for African American homebuyers, these programs were sometimes not attuned to other issues facing these homebuyers.

Credit

As I discussed in Chapter 3, the credit system can be opaque and it can take a long time to bring up scores. It's not obvious to people what things can hurt their score. And, mistakes that were made knowingly or unknowingly seven years ago can affect their scores today. For instance, Ava explained:

> Lenders, they'll tell you a little bit like, "Oh, you need to improve your credit, and you're like okay." And then what? Like well, how do I do that? Especially if I have things I can't really dispute. I did make those late payments, and if they were within the seven years, so they're not coming off.

She laughed and added, "I was like, I've got to wait seven years to get a house?" In addition to mistakes like late payments, many buyers' credit suffered from simply not having enough credit history. The credit system creates a catch-22. If you don't utilize credit perfectly, your score will suffer, but if you decide to avoid problems like late payments by not using credit at all, your score will suffer from lack of utilization. It's a tricky system that requires a lot of knowledge and discipline to do correctly. It's particularly harsh on working-class families who have been left with very little safety net. Credit has become the alternative safety net for many families. Kristin Seefeldt (2016) has found that since government social safety net programs have been scaled back, low-income families often find themselves relying on consumer debt to get through difficult times. The aspiring middle-class families I studied had sometimes found themselves in similar situations in the past.

School Loans

Many of the homebuyers had attended some college, but their road to higher education and through higher education was often disjointed and complicated. Some had been in and out of different colleges as they tried to balance family obligations and work with school. Some tried online programs and found them difficult to stick with. As a result, many were carrying debt for degrees that they never finished or had degrees that cost them more than they should have.

Taxes

The south suburbs, which are predominately Black, have higher taxes than the north suburbs, which are predominately White. The suburbs with the highest tax rates in Cook County are Ford Heights (34%), Park Forest (34%), and Riverdale (29%). They are all south of the city. The lowest tax rates are in Hinsdale (7%), Burr Ridge (7%) and Barrington (7%) (Shields and Scalzitti 2018). Hinsdale and Burr Ridge are to the far west of the city and Barrington is north west. According to the 2017 American Community Survey, each of these low-tax suburbs are over 80% non-Hispanic White (Barrington 92%, Hinsdale 86%, and Burr Ridge 83%). The highest-tax suburbs are all over 60% non-Hispanic Black (Ford Heights 94%, Park Forest 65%, and Riverdale 94%) (US Census Bureau 2017). In short, Black families are bearing the brunt of the highest taxes in the region. The areas suffering from this problem are both places where African Americans are more likely to live and where they are more likely to move. While their overall tax bills may not be as high as in areas with higher property values, it means that a greater percentage of their monthly payments go to taxes and not to building savings in home equity. Paying such high percentages as taxes is just one way in which homeownership costs African Americans more.

The homebuyers were aware of the fact that some suburbs had very high property taxes. Many mentioned struggling to find the right home because the south suburbs, where they were looking, have such high taxes. Sasha, who worked for the government of one south suburb, gave me her take on why the Southland has a problem with taxes:

> A lot of people blame it on economic development. I mean, for example, Olympia Fields is a very nice community, but it is strongly residential. They don't have a whole lot of businesses in Olympia Fields, but it's a nice place to live, but their taxes are really high. And, some of the communities are struggling where they can't get economic development, but the community is not stable, so it's not a community that you would necessarily, if you had the resources, choose to live in, so it kind of goes one way or the other. It's a few communities of kind of in the middle, and I don't know, and sometimes people just think in general that the south suburbs doesn't get the same consideration as some of the other communities on the other sides of town, like up north, or further west.

It seems that Sasha has identified an important part of the problem when she talks about retail. When a municipality has more businesses to tax, it can put less of the tax burden on homeowners and still provide the same services. When she says the south suburbs don't get "the same consideration," this appears to be true when it comes to retailers deciding where to locate. In the Chicago area, the South Suburban Coalition, which comprises the suburbs of Matteson, Olympia Fields, Park Forest, and Richton Park, all relatively high-income majority African American suburbs, conducted a study with the University of Illinois at Chicago, which suggests that race may be a key factor in retailers' decisions not to locate in these areas (Teska Associates Inc et al. 2012).

Conclusion

While homebuyers who were able to purchase homes reported satisfaction with their houses in the months after their move, the places that they moved to seem quite precarious when it comes to the things that they desire: neighborhood amenities, racial diversity, and rising home values. In many ways, one can look at this process and see how, as others have found, African Americans remain stuck in neighborhoods that are relatively disadvantaged (Sampson 2012; Sharkey 2013). Speaking to homebuyers like Kimberly and Tiffany about their family stories, we see how a cycle continues that persistently disadvantages African Americans who are striving for the American Dream, seeking out diverse areas, and generally doing everything expected from them in the terms of the ideology. On the other hand, there were the many homebuyers who were still struggling and not able to purchase after years of trying. And a few who, seeing the precarity of their potential destinations, became disenchanted with the options and decided that buying a home was not the best choice for them after all.

References

Anderson, Matthew B., and Carolina Sternberg. 2013. "'Non-White' Gentrification in Chicago's Bronzeville and Pilsen: Racial Economy and the Intraurban Contingency of Urban Redevelopment." *Urban Affairs Review* 49(3): 435–467. https://doi.org/10.1177/1078087412465590.

Clergé, Orly. 2019. *The New Noir: Race, Identity, and Diaspora in Black Suburbia.* Berkeley: University of California Press.

Freeman, Lance. 2011. *There Goes the 'Hood: Views of Gentrification from the Ground Up.* Philadelphia: Temple University Press.

Howell, Junia, and Elizabeth Korver-Glenn. 2020. "The Increasing Effect of Neighborhood Racial Composition on Housing Values, 1980–2015." *Social Problems* spaa033: 1–21. https://doi.org/10.1093/socpro/spaa033.

Moore, Natalie Y. 2016. *The South Side: A Portrait of Chicago and American Segregation.* New York: Macmillan.

Sampson, Robert J. 2012. *Great American City: Chicago and the Enduring Neighborhood Effect.* Chicago: The University of Chicago Press.

Seefeldt, Kristin S. 2016. *Abandoned Families: Social Isolation in the Twenty-First Century.* New York: Russell Sage Foundation.

Shapiro, Thomas M. 2004. *The Hidden Cost of Being African American: How Wealth Perpetuates Inequality.* New York: Oxford University Press.

Sharkey, Patrick. 2013. *Stuck in Place: Urban Neighborhoods and the End of Progress Toward Racial Equality.* Chicago: University of Chicago Press.

Shields, Nick, and James Scalzitti. 2018. "2017 Cook County Tax Rates Released." Chicago: Real Estate and Tax Service.

Teska Associates Inc., UIC Nathalie P. Voorhees Center, Business Districts Inc., and Clark Hill PLC. 2012. "South Suburban Retail Investment Study." Chicago: South Suburban Coalition.

US Census Bureau. 2010. "Census 2010." Social Explorer Tables. US Census Bureau and Social Explorer.

———. 2017. "ACS 2017 (5-Year Estimates)." Social Explorer Tables. US Census Bureau and Social Explorer.

Voorhees Center for Neighborhood and Community Improvement. 2014. "The Socioeconomic Change of Chicago's Community Areas (1970–2010)." Chicago: University of Illinois at Chicago.

7

CONCLUDING DISCUSSION

Working-class African American homebuyers are deeply interested in improving their neighborhood context. Additionally, they often believe intrinsically in the value of racially diverse neighborhoods and that racially diverse areas will be better places to raise children. At the same time, Black homebuyers must contend with the fact that neighborhoods are changing around them. The landscape of racial segregation forms a structure that is at odds with their goals, inspired by the American Dream.

The homebuyers felt that an important part of the promise of the American Dream is that hard work should buy them a place in a racially diverse, middle-class community. To be sure, these homebuyers were interested in integration, but on their own terms. They sought integrated communities where they could, as Marcus Anthony Hunter and Zandria Robinson (2018) have put it, "be Black and be free." Homeownership symbolizes success, responsibility, respectability, and freedom. They felt that under the terms of the American Dream, the success of homeownership also indicates progress towards racial equality. These homebuyers were not only interested in the moral value attached to homeownership as the fulfillment of the American Dream, but also for the financial benefits.

The obstacles that created a delay in homeownership were particularly frustrating to African Americans with a profound belief in homeownership as a symbol of achieving the dream and gaining full acceptance and equality in mainstream American life. These delays also created practical challenges for growing and aging families. In particular, families with children had to develop strategies for decoupling home and school choice, as they waited—often for years as opposed to months—to be able to move to the kinds of areas they desired.

Despite these challenges, homebuyers' profound adherence to the ideology of the American Dream encourages belief in their own agency, their own ability to break through these structural constraints. In some ways, many of the aspiring homebuyers did overcome odds to meet their goals, or at least aspects of their goals. Those who were able to purchase a home felt fulfilled in that achievement and thought that homeownership would improve their lives. At the same time, neighborhood contexts remained very similar for these households who were desperately seeking change.

As African Americans are seldom able to change their own neighborhood context for the better, the irony is that part of the challenge is actually dealing with the changes that are happening in neighborhoods. While the dynamics of racial segregation and disadvantaged neighborhoods are enduring, the demographics of specific places change. In the face of this uncertainty, homebuyers relied on search heuristics, which unfortunately often led to the unintended consequences of purchasing homes in areas that were segregated and likely to remain that way or areas that were resegregating. The homebuyers had seen their parents and grandparents struggle in declining neighborhoods, suffering from the effects of White flight and disinvestment. Those same parents and grandparents had once been pioneers, moving in order to improve their circumstances and achieve a vision of a more integrated and equitable country. These cyclical changes create a landscape where African Americans have to move geographically just to stay in places that are as desirable in terms of the neighborhood context. Whole families are running on a metaphoric treadmill, grasping for the American Dream that remains out of reach, while one misstep can send them flying backwards.

The interviews for this book were conducted in the wake of the foreclosure crisis, which exacerbated the Black–White homeownership gap and further entrenched racial inequalities in housing. We now face a crisis with social, economic, health, and racial injustice dimensions—the coronavirus pandemic. The full effects of this crisis remain to be seen, but we can anticipate racial inequity will be evident in the homeownership effects, just as we have seen in the health effects (Neal and McCargo 2020).

The emergency response to the foreclosure crisis has taken attention and resources away from assistance aimed at helping individuals make integrative moves. Subsidized rental housing also continues to be placed in predominately Black areas, exacerbating the racial segregation of low- and middle-income African Americans. As an alternative, pro-integrative features could be added to existing programs that subsidize housing for renters and homeowners. Successful pro-integrative programs such as those in Oak Park, Illinois and Shaker Heights, Ohio demonstrate that interventions can change prevailing racial dynamics and an outcome of resegregation is not inevitable. These programs, which are intended to ameliorate the effects of the foreclosure crisis and offer more affordable housing overall, could also have a goal of avoiding further resegregation, since these goals are not necessarily at odds with each other.

Additionally, while homeownership is important for reasons that extend beyond the financial, it would make sense for policy makers to pay more attention to other ways to increase upward mobility. Due to the centrality of the home to understandings of the American Dream, homeownership assistance should not be neglected. Expanding access to other forms of asset building could help all Americans, especially African Americans who have long suffered losses due to racial segregation and resulting disparities in home appreciation. New programs could make it possible for lower- and middle-income households to build their savings in more reliable assets. This kind of program would buffer African Americans from some of the financial harms caused by racial segregation. It may even be that White Americans would be more amenable to racially diverse neighborhoods if they had more diversified assets because this would lessen some of the anxiety over real-estate appreciation.

One of the appealing things about the homebuyer assistance programs to the recipients of these benefits is that, unlike other forms of assistance, they confer respectability. These programs help their recipients achieve a desired social status—that of homeowner. This homeowner status is associated with middle-class respectability and the achievement of the American Dream. I believe that it is possible for other forms of asset-building assistance to also provide a sense of acceptance, equality, and full membership in society. In creating new programs that expand efforts to build wealth, particularly for African Americans, we must pay attention to both the financial and the socio-psychological effects of these programs. Homeownership assistance helps people gain a foothold in the middle class that can provide greater financial stability and holistic well-being. But, if homeownership is available to African Americans only in precarious, segregated or resegregating neighborhoods, the gains from homeownership will be ephemeral. Racial injustice in the area of housing persists, and it contributes to the racial wealth gap and inequality in neighborhood contexts. Both neighborhood inequality and the wealth gap are serious problems for African American families. I argue that policy efforts in this area should address two goals simultaneously: desegregation of neighborhoods, and creating new opportunities for African Americans to build wealth.

I make several policy suggestions below, but I am also sensitive to the fact that the massive structural problem of racial segregation and racial injustice in housing markets will not be solved by a few housing tweaks. The kind of radical change that will be required to undo this entrenched system of inequality will require a paradigm shift. The related problem of affordable housing is also too entrenched to be solved by small policy changes. In *Manufactured Insecurity: Mobile Home Parks and Americans' Tenuous Right to Place*, Esther Sullivan (2018) argues that to really undo the structural disadvantage in our housing system, we must shift the discourse in the US and recognize housing as a human right. In addition to recognizing housing as a human right, I think that we need the paradigm shift that Richard Rothstein (2017) calls for: to recognize that racial segregation is a badge of slavery that the United States is constitutionally and morally obligated to remove.

One major challenge to addressing both of these issues, affordable housing and racial segregation, is that housing is bundled with the most widespread and consequential investment strategy for the American middle class. There is a fundamental tension between affordable housing and housing as an investment. Buying a home is an inherently risky investment strategy for middle-class families, because it requires putting all of your resources into one asset. For this strategy to make sense, that one asset has to be nearly guaranteed to increase in value faster than inflation. In other words, for homeownership to work as a mass investment strategy, housing must become more expensive over time (at a relatively quick pace) and of course, that eventually makes it unaffordable for new homebuyers (Hertz 2015). To really tackle issues of access to fair and affordable housing, we need to rethink this relationship between building the financial security of the middle class and leveraged investments in homeownership. Ultimately, this link between finance, housing, and the middle class is at the core of the contemporary American Dream, so this change will require not just new tools to build economic security for the non-rich, but a paradigm shift in our conception of the American Dream ideology.

Housing Policy to Further Integration

Pro-Integrative Policy Programs

A few policies have been used to promote integrative residential relocation, including affirmative marketing and financial incentives (Relman et al. 2010). Affirmative marketing consists of publicizing housing opportunities to racial groups most underrepresented in that area. This type of program has been implemented by public and private organizations. For example, the South Suburban Housing Center (SSHC) bought homes in a predominately Black section of Park Forest, Illinois. While making the homes available to all interested buyers, they attempted special outreach to White homebuyers (purchasing advertisements in newspapers with a predominately White circulation area).

Another approach that has been attempted involves financial incentives. The nonprofit Fund for the Future of Shaker Heights created a mortgage assistance program in a suburb of Cleveland that incentivized integrative moves. The program offers mortgage assistance to White people buying in parts of Shaker Heights where Whites are underrepresented, and to African Americans buying in parts of the town where African Americans are underrepresented (Keating 1994). These types of financial incentives and affirmative marketing policies do not run afoul of antidiscrimination laws. On the other hand, communities have had mixed results when implementing these kinds of policies. Park Forest has experienced a large decline in its White population; as of 2010, it was 60% Black. By contrast, Shaker Heights appears to be having more success with maintaining racial integration and was 37% Black in 2010 (US Census Bureau 2010). Timing and cooperation across different levels of government and community organizations are important for successful pro-integration programs.

Legal challenges have been presented to many of the available strategies for pro-integrative policy (Relman et al. 2010). Of these pro-integrative policies, quotas are the most legally questionable and have been struck down in a number of instances. In *United States v. Starrett City Associates* (1988), the court decided that a racial quota system intended to prevent racial tipping in an apartment complex in New York violated the goal of nondiscrimination because it effectively limited the number of minorities who could rent in that building.[1] The courts have given greater leeway to public entities that engaged in previous discrimination and have upheld more flexible, race-conscious programs. For instance, in *Schmidt v. Boston Housing Authority* (1981), a Massachusetts state court determined that the Boston Housing Authority could give priority to applicants who would be moving into buildings where they would be underrepresented owing to past segregation.[2] Affirmative marketing has also been determined to be legal in many cases. In *Steptoe v. Beverly Area Planning Association* (1987), the court upheld a program that provided information about housing to individuals who had stated a willingness to make integrative moves.[3] The court decided that this program does not constitute racial steering because information is available from other sources for those who want to make nonintegrative moves, and this program only increased the supply of information.

Furthermore, the group in question was not actually involved in the sale or leasing of homes. In another case involving an entity that was selling property, *South Suburban Housing Center v. Greater Suburban Board of Realtors* (1991), realtors challenged SSHC's affirmative marketing program for homes that the organization had bought in a predominately Black neighborhood.[4] The program entailed making special outreach efforts to White buyers for these homes. Since anyone regardless of race was able to buy the homes, the court determined that this program still provides equal opportunity while also encouraging integration. On the other hand, the court also determined that the Board of Realtors was not required to cooperate with the plan. Additionally, the legality of Oak Park's equity insurance program was challenged and upheld by the courts (Keating 1994). There are fewer instances of financial incentive programs, so the law is less clear on this type of program. Regardless, the general principles apply that if integrative programs do not restrict housing choice on the basis of race, they can still be race-conscious. Affirmative marketing, financial incentives for pro-integrative moves, and equity insurance programs appear to be legally viable options to promote racial integration.

Thus, it appears that it is possible to devise policies to prevent resegregation of neighborhoods. A study of fifteen neighborhood integration maintenance projects across the country demonstrated that timely, well-organized intervention can lead to successful stable integration (Saltman 1991). The study found a few key variables that allowed for successful integration maintenance. The most successful integration maintenance programs benefited from systemwide school desegregation programs. The desegregation of schools in the surrounding area removed the stigma from schools in more integrated neighborhoods because their schools were not racially marked as distinct. In contrast, none of the neighborhoods with a concentration of public housing were able to maintain integration. Concentrated public housing undermined the affirmative marketing efforts that were typically a part of integration maintenance efforts. These cases demonstrate that coordinated intervention on the part of community organizations and local and regional government bodies can stem the tide of resegregation.

In the 1970s, Harvey Luskin Molotch (1972) argued that managed integration programs were misguided and that a better solution to the problem of racial segregation would be to address racial inequality, which he believed to be its root cause. As a result of recent research on place-based inequality, it appears that this causal link may be more complicated. This research has drawn attention to ways that racial segregation actually perpetuates racial inequality. A deeper understanding of the relationship between racial inequality and racial segregation makes it clear that tackling racial segregation is an important pathway to ameliorating racial inequality. Therefore, programs that directly address racial segregation in housing are necessary. Of course, there are real reasons to be concerned that poorly designed, race-conscious programs could unintentionally exacerbate disparities in the housing market or limit the choices of members of a racial group. Although there are limited examples of affirmative pro-integrative programs, there have been success stories. Given what we know about the deleterious effects of racial segregation and its tendency to persist, more efforts should be undertaken to experiment with affirmative policies towards racial integration.

Assets Policy

One of the consequences of racial segregation is that homes in predominately Black areas appreciate more slowly than average, which contributes to racial wealth inequality. Ultimately, the racial wealth gap also manifests itself in a variety of other racial disparities. Thomas Shapiro (2005) proposes tackling the issue of racial inequality by directly addressing wealth inequality through asset-building policies. Arguably, we already have asset-security policies that disproportionately benefit the rich. Asset accounts such as 401(k)s and IRAs allow people who already have assets to protect and maintain them with help from public subsidies through the tax system. In comparison, a more equitable asset-building policy would entail developing similar types of accounts that would help poor and lower-middle-class families build assets for things like higher education, small businesses, and homeownership. For instance, Shapiro proposes allowing renters to deduct part of their rent on their tax form and have it put into a down payment account to match their own savings. To safeguard against uses of these accounts that would disproportionately benefit the already wealthy, he recommends that only earnings be eligible for matching funds. Inherited wealth and parental financial gifts would be excluded. In theory, one of the ills of racial segregation, the racial wealth gap, could be ameliorated through asset-building programs of this type. Giving non-wealthy households the chance to build wealth through assets not tied to homeownership could help to lessen the effects of racial segregation on wealth accumulation.

Another way to address the racial wealth gap is to attempt to equalize the wealth that families are able to build through homeownership by incentivizing desegregation. Shapiro (2005) suggests that one obvious way to incentivize desegregation is to equalize public school funding, which would remove an incentive for White families to segregate themselves. He recommends increasing the portion of school funding from federal and state taxes and decreasing the portion of funding from local property taxes. In addition to taking away one of the most damaging harms of racial segregation, Shapiro believes this would remove a large part of the incentive for White families to move to predominately White areas. It remains possible that other types of policies aimed at equalizing schools could encourage integrative moves. College percent plans (for example, Texas's "Top 10 Percent Law" automatically admits students whose grade point average puts them in the top ten percent of their high school) reduce the relative attractiveness of attending schools with higher overall academic achievement (which are more likely to be predominately White and wealthy). Julie Berry Cullen, Mark Long, and Randall Reback (2013) found that shortly after the University of Texas system adopted the "Top 10 Percent Law," some students were making strategic choices between high schools, but this mostly involved attending a neighborhood school instead of a magnet school within the same district. These choices to attend a neighborhood school over a magnet school were not integrative, but it's possible that given more time under the plan, parents could start making strategic integrative moves when they buy homes earlier in their children's education.

It is possible that White families would be more willing to move to less White areas if school funding was made more equitable or if it gave them greater access to a highly ranked college, but it is by no means guaranteed. Other researchers have found that perception of school quality is associated with racial makeup, and parents make decisions about schools based on their perceptions (Lareau 2014). As long as these stereotypes persist, more direct action may be needed to desegregate schools. On the other hand, changing the funding sources for public schools to make resources more equitable would still be an improvement over the current situation for many predominately Black schools.

Providing asset-building programs to assist low-wealth households (which disproportionately characterizes African American households) to save for homeownership would be helpful, but if these funds are invested in Black communities where homes do not appreciate at comparable rates to White communities, disparities will continue to grow. As I discussed in Chapter 2, the existing landscape of racial hypersegregation in metropolitan areas like Chicago structures social ties and knowledge about places. African Americans in this kind of region have more ties to predominately Black and contiguous racially transitioning parts of the region. Without pro-integrative incentives or affirmative marketing components, it is likely that the neighborhoods where African Americans would invest their down-payment savings accounts would remain more financially precarious. The original court-ordered *Gautreaux* program is an example of a highly successful renter assistance program that promoted both racial- and class-based integration. Homeownership policy could also affirmatively address racial segregation. For example, existing homeowner assistance programs can be adapted to include financial incentives for pro-integrative moves, and affirmative marketing components could be added to home purchasing counseling.

Affirmatively Furthering Fair Housing

When the Obama administration created a rule for HUD called Affirmatively Furthering Fair Housing (AFFH), this brought racial segregation back into housing policy discussions. The rule required state and local governments to assess their progress in reducing racial segregation in order to receive federal housing funds. Under this rule, municipalities that received HUD funding had to create their own annual plans to reduce historical racial segregation and have these plans approved by HUD (Massey 2015). Many municipalities around the country began work on these plans, but the Trump administration suspended the rule in 2018 and then terminated it in 2020, effectively turning US housing policy away from addressing racial segregation. In July 2020, Trump remarked about Biden's support of AFFH: "Biden will destroy your neighborhood and your American Dream." One wonders who the "you" is that former President Trump addresses. It is clear that Trump is not speaking to working-class Black aspiring homebuyers for whom the AFFH could have helped to provide a more reliable path to the American Dream.

Under AFFH, local governments would determine their own policies for achieving the goals set out by the rule. AFFH expressly encouraged regional cooperation across education, transportation, and housing agencies when selecting sites for schools, housing projects, and transportation improvements. The goal for this regional cross-agency cooperation was to design new projects in ways that encourage integration of schools and housing. With increased suburbanization of all racial and ethnic groups, racial segregation has spread to the suburbs. Therefore, programs that address whole metropolitan regions are necessary to counter the problems of racial segregation. Ideally, AFFH would have enabled the necessary cooperation across municipalities to tackle this problem. Furthermore, one of the problems with previous attempts to implement pro-integrative housing programs is that they were usually established in places that were already transitioning from predominately White to predominately majority minority. As a result, the programs are sometimes implemented too late to be effective and can essentially limit housing choices for minorities because the only possible integrative moves to incentivize are those of White households. An affirmative marketing campaign or a program with incentives for pro-integrative moves that encompassed a whole metropolitan area could overcome both of these shortfalls.

It remains to be seen whether the Biden presidential administration will bring new HUD leadership ready to work towards greater racial justice in housing with the Obama framework or through new policy approaches.

Considering Renters and Homebuyers

When designing housing policy, one should not ignore how movers (both renters and homebuyers) develop theories about neighborhoods and act on those theories. They try to predict future changes with the resources available to them. They make decisions based on those predictions that in turn affect future neighborhood change. In other words, housing policies are always interacting with the subjective experiences and theories of movers.

Since Americans are not race-blind, housing policy that ignores racial dynamics can have the unintended effect of furthering racial segregation. While homebuyer assistance programs provide resources to middle-income African Americans that are important for expanding their access to homeownership, they ignore the racial dynamics that diminish the use value and exchange value of their homes. For obvious reasons, housing policymakers have felt a need to focus on assisting the neighborhoods that have been devastated by the foreclosure crisis. But the emergency response to the foreclosure crisis has taken attention and resources away from assistance aimed at helping individuals make integrative moves. Furthermore, subsidized rental housing continues to be placed in predominately Black areas, exacerbating the racial segregation of low- and middle-income African Americans.

As an alternative, pro-integrative features could be added to existing programs that subsidize housing for renters and homeowners. Successful pro-integrative programs such as those in Oak Park, Illinois and Shaker Heights, Ohio demonstrate that interventions can change prevailing racial dynamics and an outcome of resegregation is not inevitable. A defeatist attitude towards White flight is unwarranted given that from 1990 to 2010, there was an increase in the number of integrated neighborhoods and an increase in the number of neighborhoods that remained integrated (Ellen et al. 2012). While pro-integrative programs have been successful in some cases, their scope has been limited, and they are often implemented too late to be effective. Furthermore, since housing choice voucher and down payment assistance programs already provide subsidies, it could be possible to use these funds to encourage racially integrative moves. The programs also often require housing counseling that could include an affirmative marketing component. These programs, which are intended to ameliorate the effects of the foreclosure crisis and offer more affordable housing, could also aim to avoid further resegregation, since these goals are not necessarily at odds with each other.

Reparations

This book contributes to growing understanding of why action on racial housing segregation is urgently needed. Ta-Nehisi Coates (2014) has argued that reparations are required to right the wrongs not just of slavery but of the post-slavery plunder from Black families through discriminatory housing practices. Rothstein (2017) has made a compelling case for the legal argument that racial segregation of housing is a badge of slavery, one that persists because of government action, and therefore the current state of racial segregation is *de jure* and unconstitutional.

To remedy the wrongs of racial segregation, the work ahead must permeate social, financial, and legal systems entrenched in racism. This book provides some insight into how these structural barriers are experienced by African Americans. For Black homebuyers to have full access to integrated neighborhoods, it will take more than the existing, on-their-face race-neutral, homebuyer assistance programs. We need a massive sea change in our approach to housing and we need to directly address racial injustice.

This study of homebuyers demonstrates how working-class African Americans who were deliberately and actively trying to access more integrated neighborhoods were often unable to achieve their stated goals. These homebuyers have some resources and they sought out housing counseling. We might expect homebuyers in this group to be able to overcome patterns of segregation. Even for homebuyers with financial resources and assistance, though, the structure of racial segregation limits their agency in housing choices. While African Americans have seen some success and improvement in homeownership attainment and neighborhood context, this remains far too limited. For this group, achievement of the American Dream remains precarious at best.

Ultimately, working-class African American homebuyers are being taxed for their deep belief in the American Dream. Furthermore, it's not only African Americans who are negatively affected by the pursuit of the American Dream of homeownership. There are fundamental problems with our system that bundles up housing—the main strategy to build middle-class wealth, access to shelter, and cultural recognition as a fully realized citizen—into one asset that hurts so many kinds of vulnerable people. The American Dream is attractive and alluring because many aspects of this ideology support people's well-being and flourishing. Working-class Black homebuyers are drawn to ideals of freedom and community, and want a home to be a base to engage the world where they can be secure, free, and autonomous. We need a reimagining of the American Dream, a cultural shift to help us to separate from an economic approach that is predicated on many people losing such a high-risk game, and to affirm aspects of this ideology that are important for people's well-being and flourishing.

Notes

1 United States v. Starrett City Associates, 840 F.2d 1096 (2d Cir. 1988).
2 Schmidt v. Boston Housing Authority, 505 F. Supp. 988 (D.Mass. 1981).
3 Steptoe v. Beverly Area Planning Association, 674 F. Supp. 1313 (N.D. Ill. 1987).
4 South Suburban Housing Center v. Greater Suburban Board of Realtors, 935 F.2d 868 (7th Cir. 1991).

References

Coates, Ta-Nehisi. 2014. "The Case for Reparations." The Atlantic, June 15, 2014. www.theatlantic.com/magazine/archive/2014/06/the-case-for-reparations/361631/.

Cullen, Julie Berry, Mark C. Long, and Randall Reback. 2013. "Jockeying for Position: Strategic High School Choice under Texas' Top Ten Percent Plan." *Journal of Public Economics* 97: 32–48. https://doi.org/10.1016/j.jpubeco.2012.08.012.

Ellen, Ingrid Gould, Keren Horn, and Katherine O'Regan. 2012. "Pathways to Integration: Examining Changes in the Prevalence of Racially Integrated Neighborhoods." *Cityscape* 14(3): 33–53.

Hertz, Daniel. 2015. "American Housing Policy's Two Basic Ideas Pull Cities in Opposite Directions." The Atlantic, October 14, 2015. www.theatlantic.com/business/archive/2015/10/american-housing-policy-contradictions/410332/.

Hunter, Marcus Anthony, and Zandria F. Robinson. 2018. *Chocolate Cities: The Black Map of American Life*. Berkeley: University of California Press.

Keating, W. Dennis. 1994. *The Suburban Racial Dilemma: Housing and Neighborhoods*. Philadelphia: Temple University Press.

Lareau, Annette. 2014. "Schools, Housing, and the Reproduction of Inequality." In *Choosing Homes, Choosing Schools*, edited by A. Lareau and K. Goyette. New York: Russell Sage Foundation.

Massey, Douglas S. 2015. "The Legacy of the 1968 Fair Housing Act." *Sociological Forum* 30(S1): 571–588. https://doi.org/10.1111/socf.12178.

Molotch, Harvey Luskin. 1972. *Managed Integration: Dilemmas of Doing Good in the City*. Berkeley: University of California Press.

Neal, Michael, and Alanna McCargo. 2020. "How Economic Crises and Sudden Disasters Increase Racial Disparities in Homeownership." Washington, D.C.: Urban Institute.

Relman, John P., Glenn Schlactus, and Shalini Goel. 2010. "Creating and Protecting Pro-Integration Programs under the Fair Housing Act." In *The Integration Debate: Competing Futures for American Cities*, edited by G. Squires and C. Hartman. New York: Routledge.

Rothstein, Richard. 2017. *The Color of Law: A Forgotten History of How Our Government Segregated America*. New York: Liveright Publishing Corporation.

Saltman, Juliet. 1991. "Maintaining Racially Diverse Neighborhoods." *Urban Affairs Review* 26(3): 416–441.

Shapiro, Thomas M. 2005. *The Hidden Cost of Being African American: How Wealth Perpetuates Inequality*. New York: Oxford University Press.
Sullivan, Esther. 2018. *Manufactured Insecurity: Mobile Home Parks and Americans' Tenuous Right to Place*. Oakland, California: University of California Press.
US Census Bureau. 2010. "Census 2010." Social Explorer Tables. US Census Bureau and Social Explorer.

METHODOLOGICAL APPENDIX

This project originated from my interest in the increase in out-migration from Chicago during the 2000s. A number of local news outlets were reporting on the 2010 census and the fact that Chicago had lost 200,000 residents. When I looked further into that population drop, I found out that it was almost entirely from the African American community. At a time when discussions about cities have emphasized the problems of explosive growth and gentrification, the idea that Chicago was losing people seemed odd and difficult to explain. How could this dramatic population drop be occurring in the nation's third-largest city at a time when many observers of urban life were claiming we were in the midst of a "back to the city movement." Furthermore, the fact that in Chicago we can talk about the problem of gentrification in some areas while others are emptying out highlights the vast disparities between different portions of this city. I realized that some of the disparity between this reality and typical conversations about the fates of urban areas today has to do with race and racism. Different racial groups are having wildly different experiences in major cities like Chicago.

I had some hunches about other issues that could be related to this population drop. In particular, I wondered if the Chicago Housing Authority's Plan for Transformation was influential. On further reading, I began to consider the possibility that African American suburbanization or reverse migration to the South could be drivers of this change. I was also personally interested in fair housing, affordable housing, and the problem of racial segregation, and I was curious about what the phenomenon of out-migration from Chicago might have to do with these issues.

Over time, I began to focus the scope of this project around African American homeownership. Because I was interested in becoming more involved in the intersection between urban sociology and public policy—particularly as it relates to housing—I took a position as a research assistant at the Metropolitan Planning Council (MPC) in the summer of 2014. While I was there, I had an opportunity to talk about my ideas for this project with many policy professionals who had worked on issues related to housing in Chicago. Around the same time, I also met with Maria Krysan at the University of Illinois in Chicago, who encouraged me to focus my research on homeownership because a substantial portion of the most recent work on housing has been on renters.

Through MPC, I was able to connect with Neighborhood Housing Services of Chicago and I found out about their homebuyer education classes. I realized that this would be an excellent opportunity for me to speak to potential movers before they made a decision about a move. Through my conversations with them it seemed that two of their locations would be best suited to my interest in African Americans leaving Chicago-Roseland on the South Side of the city and East Hazel Crest in the south suburbs. Eventually, I was able to get in touch with the West Cook Homeownership Center, which offers a similar program for homebuyers in the west suburb of Oak Park.

I attended homebuyer education classes and recruited participants at these three locations. I conducted the initial interviews with homebuyers in person from October 2014 to September 2015. By recruiting from homebuyer education classes I was able to get some prospective homebuyers very early in their search process. My goal was to find out their opinions on neighborhoods and the logic of their search strategies before they made decisions on homes. For some of these homebuyers, I was able to follow them over time.

Ultimately, I collected follow-up data from thirty-eight of the homebuyers during their homebuying process. This follow-up data included in-person interviews, ethnographic observation of home viewings, and brief phone interviews. The average number of interviews I conducted with each respondent was 1.8, and the number of interviews ranged from one to five (including phone and in-person interviews). In follow-up interviews, I asked the homebuyers to describe meetings with loan officers and real estate agents, along with other activities related to homebuying. I asked questions about any changes in stated preferences for location or type of home, as well as reasons for delays in the homebuying process. In final interviews, I asked respondents to reflect on the homebuying process, describe their new home, contrast their new home and neighborhood with their former residence, and describe their level of satisfaction with the new home. I coded the interview transcripts for common themes, which were determined inductively through the research process.

I was inspired by the methodology that Herbert Gans employed in *The Levittowners*, which provided information about how the perspectives and opinions of his respondents about the new suburban development they had moved to changed over time. Gans utilized a two-year ethnographic study combined with a series of surveys and formal interviews. One of the strengths of this study is that it tracked people from before they moved into their suburban homes until they had been there for over two years, so it demonstrates how attitudes toward both their old and new homes changed after moving. One major change in attitudes between the first survey and the later interviews was that 59% of the women who had lived in Philadelphia before said that they would like to move back to the city "were it not for the children," which is three times as many as gave that answer in the mail questionnaire before they moved; only 29% of men answered in the affirmative the second time, which constituted only a small increase from the previous survey (Gans 1982). If the study had consisted only of the survey conducted after participants had lived in their new home for two years, one may have erroneously concluded that space or resources for child-rearing was the primary motivation for choosing a home in Levittown.

Karyn Lacy's research on middle-class suburban African Americans is one of the closest precursors to this work, but she was only able to gain her participants' attitudes about their neighborhoods after they had been living in these areas for some time. She asked her respondents what they appreciated about their neighborhood, but we do not know whether their answers convey the reasons that they reside in those locations. For instance, Lacy found that her subjects sometimes experienced discrimination when looking for a home, and this may have influenced where they moved, but the participants in her study tended to de-emphasize that aspect of the moving process. Additionally, racial steering is not always visible to victims when it occurs (that is, prospective buyers do not know about the homes they were not shown). Lacy also conducted participant observation research on the real estate market in the area. When she posed as a potential homebuyer in this region, she found evidence of subtle racial steering and the marketing of particular communities to Black people (Lacy 2007). Understandably, her participants preferred not to dwell on opportunities that may have been denied to them for reasons of racial discrimination and instead focused on the fact that they were satisfied with the homes that they chose, much like my respondents did.

The homebuyers in this study are a very particular population because they all attended homebuyer education seminars. Both Neighborhood Housing Services (NHS) of Chicago and the West Cook Homeownership Center (WCHC) are certified by the Department of Housing and Urban Development to provide housing counseling. The homebuyer education seminar offered by NHS and WCHC is a prerequisite for a homeownership education certificate, which some lenders require before issuing certain loans. Receiving this certificate can also make some buyers eligible for specific government subsidies when purchasing a home. NHS is also an official partner of NeighborWorks America, originally called Neighborhood Housing Services, which began as a grassroots community organization in Pittsburgh in 1971 with the goal of revitalizing declining inner-city neighborhoods. There are now about 250 local NeighborWorks organizations operating in all fifty states, the District of Columbia, and Puerto Rico. In 2015, NeighborWorks helped 21,700 families become homeowners through their programs including prepurchase education. NeighborWorks clients differ from the general population of homebuyers in that they are disproportionately African American, Hispanic, low-income, and female (Li et al. 2016). It is also possible that these homebuyers, having benefited from the class, are better prepared for the home search than other similar prospective homebuyers would be. While this may make this sample less like the general population of homebuyers, it likely means that this study underestimates the challenges facing working-class African Americans trying to buy homes.

This opportunity to interview potential homebuyers during their search for a home gave the project a deeper focus on homeownership. Through my interviews and the time I spent at the homebuyer education classes, I learned how central the goal of homeownership itself was to the housing decisions of my respondents. Homeownership is seen as intrinsically valuable and it can actually be its own motivation for relocation. Furthermore, the population at these seminars tended to be lower middle-income or working-class, so this led me to focus on how these individuals were attempting to gain a stronger hold on middle-class status.

For a comparison group, I conducted interviews with seven neighbors of the homebuyers, people who lived within 200 feet of a homebuyer's origin address. Using the homebuyers whose original addresses were within the city of Chicago, I used ArcGIS, a mapping and geographic data analysis software program, to develop a list of residents who lived within a 200-foot radius of their initial address. I sent letters to the residents at these 909 addresses, and I called some of these residents where publicly listed phone numbers were available. I sent these letters in August 2015. From this list, I was able to conduct interviews with seven neighbors of the homebuyers from August 2015 to September 2015. I conducted the interviews in person, at subjects' homes or another location of their choosing. The interviews covered their perceptions of their home, neighborhood, and the city of Chicago. I also asked about their lifetime history of moves and if they had any plans or desire to move in the future.

I found that the neighbors had very similar things to say about their neighborhoods as the homebuyers. For instance, Grace was in her eighties and was living in Chicago in the home her parents had bought in the 1950s. At the time that her parents bought the home, it was a mostly White neighborhood, but today it is an almost all-Black neighborhood. She had noticed other changes in the neighborhood more recently. Like many of the aspiring homebuyers, Grace complained that some new neighbors did not adhere to middle-class norms. She was particularly incensed about men who were hanging out on her street:

> They're not teenagers, they're not 19. They're 37, 35, but they cuss [...] all day long for the last four years, and we have called the police. Some of the answers from the police are very cruel to a person who needs help. The answers were, "Well, they're not killing nobody, miss." They started cooking in front of the yard. We had never had that [before]—cooking out in front. Well, they say that they had meetings with Section 8 people [about] how

> [to] live with people that own. People that own know how to take care of their yard and grass. You have to learn how to live with these people.

Like the homebuyers, Grace believes that a large number of housing voucher recipients moving to her neighborhood has caused neighborhood decline. She also believes that homeowners make better neighbors than renters, because they are more likely to adhere to middle-class norms, including using the backyard and not the front for recreation. I heard similar ideas about homeownership from the other neighbors, even neighbors who currently rent. Also, the neighbors who were not yet homeowners expressed interest in owning a home eventually. All of this suggests that the prospective homebuyers recruited from the homebuyer education classes are not a particularly odd group in terms of their perspective on the neighborhoods they were trying to leave or their desire for homeownership.

References

Gans, Herbert J. 1982. *The Levittowners: Ways of Life and Politics in a New Suburban Community*. New York: Columbia University Press.

Lacy, Karyn. 2007. *Blue-Chip Black: Race, Class, and Status in the New Black Middle Class*. Berkeley: University of California Press.

Li, Wei, Bing Bai, Laurie Goodman, and Jun Zhu. 2016. "NeighborWorks America's Homeownership Education and Counseling: Who Receives It and Is It Effective?" Washington, D.C.: Urban Institute.

INDEX

Note: Page numbers in **bold** indicate tables; those in *italics* indicate figures.

For Product Safety Concerns and Information please contact our EU
representative GPSR@taylorandfrancis.com
Taylor & Francis Verlag GmbH, Kaufingerstraße 24, 80331 München, Germany

www.ingramcontent.com/pod-product-compliance
Ingram Content Group UK Ltd.
Pitfield, Milton Keynes, MK11 3LW, UK
UKHW022313250926
475702UK00046B/765
9780367075927